TASTY

EVERY DAY

TASTY™

EVERY DAY
all of the flavour, none of the fuss

EBURY PRESS

10 9 8 7 6 5 4 3 2 1

Published in 2019 by Ebury Press,
an imprint of Ebury Publishing,
20 Vauxhall Bridge Road, London SW1V 2SA

Ebury Press is part of the Penguin Random House
group of companies whose addresses can be found
at global.penguinrandomhouse.com

 Penguin
Random House
UK

First published by Clarkson Potter in 2019
This edition first published by Ebury Press in 2019

www.penguin.co.uk

A CIP catalogue record for this book is available from the British Library

TASTY is a trademark of BuzzFeed, Inc., and used under license. All rights
reserved. Some recipes originally appeared on Tasty.co.

Library of Congress Cataloging-in-Publication Data

ISBN 9781785039454

Colour origination by Rhapsody Ltd, London
Printed and bound in Italy by L.E.G.O. S.p.A

 MIX
Paper from
responsible sources
FSC® C018179

Penguin Random House is committed to
a sustainable future for our business, our
readers and our planet. This book is made
from Forest Stewardship Council®
certified paper.

CONTENTS

WELCOME TO YOUR NEW EVERY DAY

We know you're busy, so we'll make it quick. Or, actually: *You'll* make it quick. Tasty is all about giving you the tools to make every meal a celebration—even at the end of a long day, when the couch is more appealing than the stove. That's why the recipes in this book are not only delicious, but also fast and easy. We think the term *every day* has gotten a bum rap, so we're reclaiming weeknight dinners with dishes that are anything but average. With these seventy-seven recipes, created with your busy schedule in mind, cutting to the chase has never tasted so good.

Here at the Tasty kitchen, we love creating over-the-top desserts and party-ready appetizers, but we're equally obsessed with creating the food that powers commutes and community organizing, work-study and workouts, parent-teacher conferences and parents-who-can't-even, jobs and second jobs—the stuff of every day. So whether you're a seasoned cook looking to add to your stable of go-tos or a novice chef who just wants some answers to the eternal question of "What's for dinner?" *Tasty Every Day* is here to make every day tasty.

Designed for You

We designed this book to make your life easier. So whether you're short on time, ingredients, or clean pans, there's a chapter in here for you. If the thought of a sink full of dirty dishes is enough to make you lose your appetite (honestly, same), flip on over to one pot/pan meals, where you'll find recipes that are short on cookware casualties and long on flavor. From Spaghetti with Caramelized Lemon, Shrimp, and Parsley (page 28) to Easy-Peasy Potato Curry (page 23), these one-pot wonders will spare your sink and spoil your taste buds. Does the idea of coming home from work to a hot meal make you feel all fancy? Then it's the slow cooker to the rescue, with Tuscan White Bean Soup (page 34) that cooks itself while you get that bread. Or if you're ready to take that Instant Pot for a spin and need some help making the most of it, Pot Roast with Mashed Cauliflower (page 46) and Creamy Chickpea Stew with Chiles and Cilantro (page 49) will be your instant favorites.

When your cupboards are looking a little bare, check out five-ingredient (or fewer!) meals that are full of flavor, like BBQ Chicken–Stuffed Sweet Potatoes (page 62) and Cauliflower Mac 'n' Cheese (page 61). If you're shouting "Time is of the essence!" (to yourself, in the kitchen), you'll want to take a look at meals you can make in 20 minutes max—like Beef and Broccoli Noodle Stir-Fry (page 82), Vegan Fettuccine Alfredo (page 83), and Fancy Lamb Chops with Crispy Potatoes and Mint Salad (page 89). That's right: dinner in less time than it takes to decide what to watch on Netflix.

When you crave the taste of takeout without the blow to your bank account, take(out) matters into your own hands with Baked

Potato and Pea Dinner Samosas (page 92) or Easy General Tso's Chicken (page 111) that's way better than just tso-tso. Okay, okay: We get that sometimes, no matter *how* easy the recipe is, the idea of turning on your oven at all is about as appealing as going out hunting and gathering after a hard day—which is why we've got a whole chapter of recipes you don't have to cook at all, like Avocado Toast, 4 Ways (page 122)—played-out millennial jokes not included—and Curried Rotisserie Chicken Waldorf Salad (page 124).

Sitting around the table for a relaxing, unplugged meal every day sounds great, but let's be real: the road to grabbing a cup of yogurt and calling it dinner is paved with good intentions. Enter: bowl and handheld meals— Hearty Fall Harvest Bowl (page 148) and Chicken, Broccoli, and Cheddar Pockets (page 160), the perfect on-the-go eats for when life gets in the way of a sit-down meal. And when you just want something delicious to munch on or a sweet treat to cap off the day? BAM: Check out snacks and noshes. Sure, you *could* still go for that yogurt, but we have a feeling you're going to want to add some Maple-Cinnamon Trail Mix (page 178), or better yet, swap that yogurt out for some Coconut Chia Pudding (page 176).

Every day is different, which is why we've created *a lot* of different kinds of delicious.

Make It Meal Prep

If you're already a Tasty fan (hi, we love you!), you know we're all about making every meal moment of "yesssss," but we're also about creating recipes that work for you—even on the days when you don't have a moment to spare. That's where meal prepping—or, as we like to call it, the gift you give your future self—comes

in. And if we do say so ourselves, the recipes in this book make *excellent* gifts—we designed them with meal prep in mind.

Every chapter here begins with a call to Make It Meal Prep, which features a recipe for a delicious, versatile dish along with four different (and super simple!) ways to eat it. So you can have your zucchini fritters (see page 76) and eat them (for four meals), too!

Handy Tools

Here at Tasty, we don't think you need an arsenal of professional-grade kitchen tools to cook seriously delicious food. If you've got some, awesome (also—can we borrow your strawberry huller?). But if you're a little light in the gadget department, fear not. There's no need to blow your budget (or create a fake wedding registry!) to stock your kitchen, but we do have recommendations for a few tools that will make the recipes in this book even easier and faster. If you're feeling overwhelmed with all the options out there, Tasty's line of kitchenware—which you can find at Walmart stores and online—has great, inexpensive versions of a lot of these.

Slow cooker: If you're short on time, this little buddy will be an invaluable addition to your kitchen (especially if you're eyeing the slow cooker recipes in this book). A slow cooker allows you to prepare food at a low temperature and—you guessed it!—slowly. One of our favorite things about it is that you truly can set it and forget it. You don't even need to be in the house while it's doing its thing, making it perfect for anyone with a busy schedule. And just to (slowly) sweeten the deal, you can get a basic, functional slow cooker for under $30.

Multipurpose cooker: Much like Tasty chefs, multipurpose cookers are culinary jacks-of-all-trades. While some are heavier on the bells and whistles than others (oh hello, yogurt maker), most multi-cookers—including the ubiquitous favorite, the Instant Pot—will be able to pressure cook, steam, sauté, sear, *and* slow cook. Pressure cooking—a technique called for in some of our recipes—uses steam's pressure to raise the boiling temperature of water so that food cooks much faster, while at the same time forcing more liquid into whatever you're cooking. TLDR: If your favorite kind of meat is "falling off the bone," you're gonna love the pressure cooker. Besides making short work of tough meat, pressure cooking is also a quick way to cook rice, beans, and even hard-boiled eggs. We think we're in love.

Chef's knife: If you're going to buy one knife, a chef's knife is the way to go. It's incredibly versatile—you'll use it for everything from chopping veggies to carving up a chicken. A chef's knife can cost anywhere from $15 to thousands of dollars (seriously!), but the most important consideration in buying a knife is how it feels in your hand. It's best to try before you buy so you can be sure the knife you pick feels good in your hand. Just like with work and life, or your bank account, balance is key. A good way to test a knife's balance is to hold it in your hand and loosen your grip slightly—a well-balanced knife won't tip forward immediately.

No matter how fancy your knife, it's important to keep it sharp. Not to put too fine a point on it, but if your blade is dull, things could get a little . . . dicey. It might sound counterintuitive, but a sharp knife is much safer than a dull one, because it's more precise and less likely to skid and slip, taking out a finger as it

goes down. TBH, a sharp knife makes cutting faster, too. Many kitchen stores will sharpen your knives for you, or if you prefer to DIY, you can purchase a sharpening device or stone. Additionally, you can ensure your knives are smooth by using a honing steel to keep the blades centered and straight.

Stainless-steel grater: Don't leave your grater in the drawer until it's time to shred cheese—it'll get provolonely! Amazing cheese jokes aside, you'll be missing out on a great kitchen hack: instead of mincing your ginger and garlic with a knife, you can use a box grater or a Microplane to get the job done more quickly. (Pro tip: Store your ginger in the freezer to make the job even easier.)

Kitchen tongs: Tongs will make just about any kind of cooking easier. Think of them as a smaller—and more heat-resistant—set of hands, ready to help you with everything from flipping meat to tossing pasta to grabbing the paprika off a high shelf (okay, that last one depends on your level of dexterity). Make sure you buy a pair with scalloped edges—the better to grip you with, my dear!

Dutch oven: A Dutch oven is a large lidded pot, usually enameled cast iron, which you can use on the stovetop or stick in the oven or even do both in the same recipe. They're perfect for making casseroles, soups, and stews (or French Beef Chili with Red Wine, Bacon, and Onions, page 27), as well as browning meat, deep-frying, and even baking bread. Yeah, it's probably time to go Dutch.

Cast-iron skillet: We love cast-iron skillets for a few reasons. They're incredibly durable and long-lasting. If you treat your cast iron right, it will last a lifetime. That means *don't* scrub it with an abrasive pad to clean it; instead, wash it with non-soapy warm water and a stiff brush, or with kosher salt for stubborn stuck-on foods, and make sure to dry it thoroughly so it doesn't rust. They're also perfect for one-skillet recipes, because you can use 'em on the stovetop and then stick 'em right in the oven. Plus, once you build up a nice seasoning (accumulated layers of oil from cooking in the pan), cast iron is naturally nonstick. In short, when it comes to making delicious foods, cast-iron skillets are *seasoned* pros.

Rimmed baking sheet: A rimmed baking sheet is a must-have for a multitude of kitchen tests, from roasting veggies to whipping up a Taco-Night Crunch Wrap (page 104). They're fairly inexpensive, and easy to find at any kitchen supply shop or even your local supermarket. The standard size is 13 by 18 inches, and that's the size you'll see you in all the recipes in this book.

Immersion blender: Compact and powerful, the immersion blender is an all-star when it comes to making silky-smooth soups (like Spicy Butternut Squash Soup with Peanut Gremo-lata, page 44), smoothies, and even whipped cream. It's shaped like a wand, with a handle at the top and a blade at the bottom, and it's small enough to fit in a drawer (a big plus for anyone with a mini kitchen). One of the major benefits of this tool is that it can blend hot food *in the pot*, so you don't have to worry about pouring it into a countertop blender bit by bit. Less mess, more soup: That's a kitchen tool we can get behind.

Food storage containers: As we *may* already have mentioned, we're all about meal prep in the Tasty kitchen. To make your meal prepping easier, we recommend you get a variety of storage containers to keep your food fresh. Glass and plastic containers each have their advantages—glass are microwave safe and easier to keep stain-free, while plastic will be easier to transport. Of course, you could always get a combination of the two—then you'll be an unstoppable meal prepper!

Helpful Hints

Before you start cooking: Read the whole recipe. Okay, maybe this is an obvious one, but we've definitely been guilty of diving into a recipe without reading it all the way to the end—and subsequently finding ourselves stranded without a necessary tool, an ingredi-ent, or even enough time. So before you start cooking, take a moment and do a little looking.

Get to preppin': After you give your recipe a good read, it's *mise en place* time! *Mise en place* (which roughly translates from French to "everything in its place") means preparing your ingredients before you begin cooking—from chopping the vegetables to measuring out the spices. A little prep will reduce your stress level when the heat is on, and make your whole kitchen operation run more smoothly.

Spoons are appealing: Ginger is one of our favorite aromatics, but its twisty shape can sometimes make it a challenge to prep. That's why we were thrilled to learn that the very best way to peel ginger isn't with a peeler, but with a humble teaspoon. Just scrape the concave side of the spoon down the side of the ginger and watch that skin peel away.

creates steam, which prevents caramelization. Translation: No nice, crispy crust for you. Your pan shouldn't resemble the road at rush hour! Instead, cook in batches to give your food a little elbow room.

Don't flip out: Speaking of browning, moving your food around in the pan too much will also thwart the process. Unless the recipe specifies otherwise, let your meat or veggies sit undisturbed for a bit as they cook, to give them a chance to get a lil' crispy.

Waste not (pasta water), want not (flawless sauces): If you're pouring all your pasta water down the drain, you're wasting a valuable resource! Pasta water is full of salt (if you're properly salting your pasta water—which you should be!) and starch, which will help thicken your sauce. So make sure to reserve a little before you drain, and add it to the sauce in small increments when you add the pasta.

Sear genius: When you're searing meat (like for Pot Roast with Mashed Cauliflower, page 46), make sure to pat it dry with a paper towel before putting it into the pot or pan—excess moisture on the meat will cause it to steam rather than sear.

Let it rest: While we're on the subject of meat, don't forget this crucial step when cooking a piece of lamb or steak: let it rest for at least five minutes before slicing into it. Doing so allows the flavorful juices in the meat to redistribute themselves rather than leaking out all over the cutting board when you carve.

Crowd control: When you're cooking on the stovetop, overcrowding your pan will prevent your food from browning. An overcrowded pan

Clean as you go: This one's pretty self-explanatory, but still important. If you do even a little bit of cleaning here and there as you're cooking—like giving dishes and pans a quick rinse when you're done with them—you won't have a massive kitchen mess to contend with at the end of the meal. One helpful trick? Keep a designated "garbage bowl" on the counter to contain the chaos.

The most important thing to remember is that the best way to learn to cook is *to cook*. Definitely don't *not* cook because it seems hard or you feel like it's going to take too long—this book is here to rescue you from that fake news! Every meal is an opportunity to figure out what you love to eat—every single day. Go forth, Tasty chef, and carpe di-yum!

PAN

ENCHILADA RICE

Traditional enchiladas are swaddled in tortillas, but this recipe swaps wraps with rice for a hearty dish that's easy to transform into meal after meal without compromising on flavor. And if you miss the tortillas, fear not! They make an appearance on day three (or, as we like to call it, Burrito Day). This recipe also introduces one of our favorite meal prep pro tips: when in doubt, put an egg on it.

SERVES 4

<‹ • • • • • • • • • • • • • • ›>

1 tablespoon **vegetable oil**

½ cup finely chopped **red onion**

1 tablespoon minced **garlic**

1 cup finely chopped mixed green and red **bell peppers**

1 cup finely chopped **tomatoes**

1½ cups **long-grain brown rice**

1 cup canned **black beans**, drained and rinsed

1 cup canned **tomato puree**

1 tablespoon finely chopped **fresh cilantro**, plus more for garnish

1 teaspoon **chili powder**

1 teaspoon **ground cumin**

Kosher salt and **freshly ground black pepper**

½ cup shredded **Monterey Jack cheese**

½ **avocado**, pitted, peeled, and cubed

1 Preheat the oven to 400°F.

2 Heat the oil in a large cast-iron skillet over medium heat. Add the onion and garlic and cook, stirring, until soft, 3 to 4 minutes. Add the bell peppers and cook, stirring, until soft, 3 to 4 minutes. Stir in the tomatoes and cook for 1 minute. Scrape the vegetables into a bowl and set aside.

3 Return the skillet to high heat, pour in 3 cups water, and bring to a boil. Stir in the rice, reduce the heat to medium to maintain a simmer, and cook, stirring, until the water has mostly been absorbed and the rice is almost tender, 15 to 18 minutes.

4 Return the vegetables to the skillet and add the beans, tomato puree, cilantro, chili powder, and cumin. Season with salt and black pepper and stir to combine. Cover the top evenly with the cheese and bake until the rice is tender and bubbling in the center, about 25 minutes.

5 Remove the skillet from the oven, top with the avocado and more cilantro, and serve.

EAT IT FOUR DIFFERENT WAYS

MAKE IT

MEAL PREP

day ①

Serve with a side salad of chopped romaine lettuce and cherry tomatoes topped with your favorite dressing.

day ②

Spoon into taco shells and serve with sour cream, salsa, and guacamole.

Spoon into a large flour tortilla and roll up to make a burrito.

Serve in a bowl and top with a fried egg.

day ④

day ③

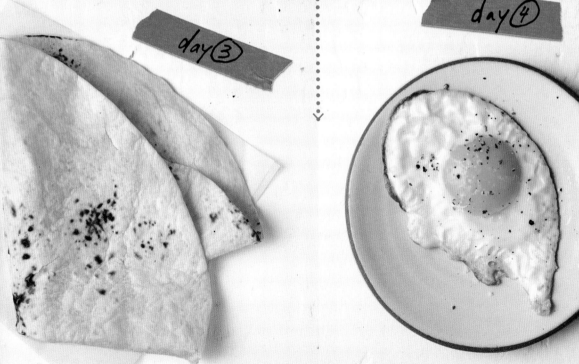

BRITISH-STYLE FISH POTPIE
WITH CIDER AND CHEDDAR

2 tablespoons **all-purpose flour**, plus more for dusting

1 (9 by 11-inch) sheet store-bought frozen **puff pastry**, thawed in the fridge overnight

3 tablespoons **unsalted butter**

1 small **yellow onion**, finely chopped

1 small **carrot**, finely chopped

1 small **celery stalk**, finely chopped

1 small **new potato**, peeled and finely diced

Kosher salt and **freshly ground black pepper**

1 cup **heavy cream**

½ cup **hard apple cider** (you can use nonalcoholic, if you like)

12 ounces skinless **cod**, **haddock**, or **other firm, white-fleshed fish**, cut into 1-inch pieces

½ cup **frozen peas**

5½ ounces **sharp Cheddar cheese**: 4 ounces cut into ½-inch cubes, 1½ ounces shredded (½ cup)

1 large **egg**, lightly beaten

If you've never met a fish potpie, we're absolutely chuffed to introduce you to this staple British comfort food—we think it's about time it swam over to this side of the pond. Fish is packed with healthy protein, and for this dish, you can use any kind of firm, white-fleshed fish you fancy. You may have heard that it's a bad idea to mix cheese and seafood, but we think that after one bite of this potpie, you'll agree that that's just an old fish tale.

1 Preheat the oven to 350°F.

2 On a flour-dusted baking sheet, roll the pastry into an 11-inch square, then trim it into an 11-inch round. Refrigerate the dough until ready to use.

3 Melt the butter in a 10-inch cast-iron or other ovenproof skillet over medium-high heat. Add the onion, carrot, celery, and potato, season with salt and pepper, and cook, stirring, until the vegetables are softened, 6 to 8 minutes. Sprinkle the flour over the vegetables and cook, stirring, to cook the raw taste out of the flour, about 1 minute. Pour in the cream and cider. Bring to a simmer, stirring, and cook until thickened, about 3 minutes more. Season the filling heavily with salt and pepper.

4 Stir in the fish and peas until evenly distributed, then scatter the cheese cubes evenly over the top (do not stir them in or press them down). Remove the skillet from the heat. Gently place the pastry round over the filling and carefully press it along the edges of the skillet with your fingers to seal. Brush the pastry with the beaten egg, then use a paring knife to cut four small slits in the top to release steam. Scatter the shredded cheese evenly over the pastry.

5 Bake the pie until the pastry is golden brown on top and the fish is cooked through, 30 to 35 minutes. Remove the pie from the oven and let cool for 10 minutes before serving.

CHICKEN POTPIE

1 tablespoon **olive oil**

1½ pounds boneless, skinless **chicken breast**, cut into ½-inch cubes

Kosher salt and **freshly ground black pepper**

½ medium **white onion**, finely chopped

2 **garlic cloves**, minced

2 cups cubed (½-inch) **Yukon Gold potatoes**

2 cups frozen **pea and carrot medley**

4 tablespoons (½ stick) **unsalted butter**

⅓ cup **all-purpose flour**

2 cups **chicken stock**

1 frozen **prepared pie crust**, thawed

1 large **egg**, beaten

Chicken potpie is the ultimate in comfort food, and since there's nothing comforting about a sink full of dishes, we've packed all the hearty goodness into a single skillet. You'll save time by using some pre-cut frozen veggies (which, side note, have the same levels of fiber, vitamins, and minerals as fresh ones—thanks, science!) and a prepared pie crust.

1 Preheat the oven to 400°F.

2 Heat the oil in a 10-inch cast-iron skillet over medium-high heat. Add the chicken, season with salt and pepper, and cook, stirring, until the meat is golden brown on the outside and no longer pink in the center, 6 to 8 minutes. Remove the chicken from the pan and set aside.

3 Return the skillet to medium heat. Add the onion and garlic and cook, stirring, until translucent, about 5 minutes. Add the potatoes and cook, stirring, for 5 minutes more. Stir in the peas and carrots, followed by the butter, allowing it to melt. Sprinkle the flour over the top, covering the vegetables, and quickly stir to avoid lumps. Pour in the stock and bring to a boil to thicken the sauce, 2 to 3 minutes. Season the filling with salt and pepper and remove the skillet from the heat.

4 Place the pie crust over the chicken-vegetable mixture and carefully press it along the edges of the skillet with your fingers to seal. Brush the pastry with the beaten egg, then use a paring knife to cut three slits in the top to release steam. Bake the chicken potpie until the crust is golden brown, 25 to 30 minutes.

5 Remove the skillet from the oven and let the potpie stand for 5 minutes before serving.

ROASTED CHICKEN
AND RAINBOW VEGETABLES

SERVES 4

12 ounces **blue fingerling potatoes**, halved lengthwise

6 ounces **green beans**, ends trimmed

3 medium **carrots**, peeled and cut diagonally into ½-inch-thick coins

6 whole **garlic cloves**, unpeeled

1 **lemon**, sliced into 6 to 8 rounds and seeds removed

½ large **purple onion**, thinly sliced crosswise

2 tablespoons **olive oil**, plus more for brushing

1 tablespoon finely chopped **fresh rosemary**

1 tablespoon finely chopped **fresh thyme**

Kosher salt and **freshly ground black pepper**

4 (8- to 10-ounce) boneless, skinless **chicken breasts**

1 teaspoon **sweet paprika**

Eating the rainbow has more benefits than just making your plate more Instagrammable (though that one's definitely up there). Apart from the visual aspect, eating a broad spectrum of veggies ensures you're getting a wide array of nutrients—which are often color-coded, because nature is just that good. This dish is an easy and delicious way to get a ton of essential vitamins (even if you're just doing it for the 'gram).

1 Preheat the oven to 375°F.

2 On a large rimmed baking sheet, arrange the potatoes, green beans, carrots, garlic, lemon, and onion in separate rows. Drizzle the olive oil and sprinkle the rosemary and thyme evenly over all the rows. Season with salt and pepper, then toss each row to coat them in the oil and seasonings, keeping each row separate. Spread the vegetables out in a single layer on the sheet, maintaining the rows and leaving a gap in the center to place the chicken.

3 Brush each chicken breast all over with more olive oil, sprinkle each with ¼ teaspoon paprika, and season both sides with salt and pepper. Place the chicken in the gap on the baking sheet, and bake until the vegetables are tender and the chicken is cooked through, 25 to 30 minutes.

EASY-PEASY
POTATO CURRY

2 tablespoons **vegetable oil**

1 medium **yellow onion**, finely chopped

4 teaspoons **curry powder**

2 teaspoons minced **fresh ginger**

2 teaspoons **ground cumin**

1½ teaspoons **sweet paprika**

1 teaspoon **cayenne**

½ teaspoon **ground allspice**

4 **garlic cloves**, minced

2 pounds **russet potatoes**, peeled and cut into ½-inch cubes

1 (15-ounce) can **chickpeas**, drained and rinsed

2 teaspoons **kosher salt**

Freshly ground black pepper

1 cup **vegetable stock**

1 tablespoon **lemon juice**

1 (14-ounce) can diced **tomatoes**

1 (14-ounce) can **unsweetened coconut milk**

Chopped **fresh cilantro**, for garnish

Cooked rice and **naan bread**, for serving

Curry up! You're not going to want to wait to make this super-flavorful Indian-inspired dish. And good news for meal preppers: The aromatics (spices, ginger, garlic, and onion) in this curry will develop more fully over time, which translates to next-level leftovers.

1 Heat the vegetable oil in a large saucepan over medium heat. Add the onion and cook, stirring, until translucent, 4 to 6 minutes. Add the curry powder, ginger, cumin, paprika, cayenne, allspice, and garlic and cook, stirring, until fragrant, about 2 minutes.

2 Add the potatoes, chickpeas, and salt and season with black pepper. Stir to coat with the spices. Stir in the stock, lemon juice, tomatoes and their juices, and coconut milk. Increase the heat to high and bring to a boil. Reduce the heat to medium to maintain a simmer and cook, stirring, until the potatoes are tender and easily pierced with a fork, 20 to 25 minutes.

3 Remove the pan from the heat and sprinkle with cilantro. Serve hot, with cooked rice and naan.

BAKED SWEET ITALIAN SAUSAGES
WITH GRAPES AND GARLIC GREEN BEANS

1 pound **green grapes**, halved if large

1 pound **sweet Italian sausages** (5 or 6)

4 **thyme sprigs**

3 tablespoons **olive oil**

¼ teaspoon **crushed red pepper flakes**

Kosher salt and **freshly ground black pepper**

1 pound **green beans**, ends trimmed

2 **garlic cloves**, minced

Finely chopped **fresh flat-leaf parsley**, for serving (optional)

You might not know it yet, but sausages and grapes go together like the internet and memes. In our version of this classic Tuscan dish, the tart grapes balance the richness of the sausage, and the fresh herbs and green beans add a summery brightness. So no matter what season it is outside your kitchen, your table will feel like an Italian villa in June (you know, if you squint).

1. Preheat the oven to 425°F. Line a large rimmed baking sheet with foil.

2. In a large bowl, combine the grapes, sausages, thyme, 2 tablespoons of the olive oil, and the red pepper flakes. Season with salt and black pepper and toss to coat everything evenly with the oil.

3. Arrange the sausages on one side of the baking sheet, leaving plenty of room between each, and prick each a few times with the tines of a fork. Spread the grapes and thyme sprigs in an even layer on the opposite side of the baking sheet. Set the bowl aside (no need to wash it).

4. Bake the sausages and grapes until the grapes start to soften and the outside of the sausages is opaque, about 15 minutes.

5. In the bowl you used for the grapes and sausages, combine the green beans, the remaining 1 tablespoon olive oil, and the garlic. Season with salt and pepper and toss to coat evenly.

6. Stir the grapes, then push them over on the baking sheet to make room for the green beans. Arrange the green beans in a single layer down the center of the baking sheet. Flip the sausages and bake until the sausages are cooked through and the green beans are golden brown and tender, about 15 minutes.

7 Using tongs, transfer the sausages to a cutting board and let rest for 5 minutes. Meanwhile, discard the thyme sprigs, then divide the grapes and green beans among four serving plates, keeping them separate on the plates. Cut the sausages on an angle into ½-inch-thick slices and arrange them beside the grapes. Sprinkle with parsley, if you like, and serve.

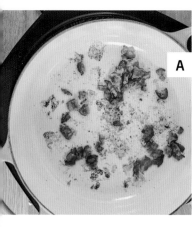

FRENCH BEEF CHILI

WITH RED WINE, BACON, AND ONIONS

4 slices **thick-cut bacon**, cut into 1-inch pieces

1 (10-ounce) package **frozen pearl onions**, thawed and dried thoroughly

1 (10-ounce) package **cremini or button mushrooms**, stemmed and quartered (about 4 cups)

Kosher salt and **freshly ground black pepper**

1½ pounds **ground beef**, preferably 80% lean

¼ cup **all-purpose flour**

1½ cups **red wine**

2 **thyme sprigs**

1 dried **bay leaf**

2 ounces **Gruyère cheese**, shredded (1 cup)

Finely chopped **fresh flat-leaf parsley**, for serving

4 (1-inch-thick) slices **sourdough bread**, toasted

We love chili so much, we thought it deserved a fancy European vacation. This chili is our take on boeuf bourguignon, a classic French stew traditionally made with chunks of beef. We swapped those out for ground beef for a quicker version that retains the rich complexity of the original. Even if a vacation's not in your future, this meal will make your day feel just a little fancier.

1   Spread the bacon in a single layer over the bottom of a large Dutch oven or saucepan and place the pot over medium heat. Once the bacon starts sizzling, cook, stirring occasionally, until it has rendered most of its fat, about 10 minutes A . Add the onions and mushrooms, season with salt and pepper, and cook, stirring occasionally, until caramelized and tender, about 20 minutes B . Using a slotted spoon, transfer the bacon and vegetables to a bowl.

2   Return the pot to medium-high heat, add the ground beef, and cook, stirring occasionally to break the meat up as much as possible, until all the liquid has evaporated and the beef is browned and caramelized, about 12 minutes. Sprinkle the flour over the beef C and stir to cook the raw taste out of the flour, about 2 minutes D . Pour in the wine and add the thyme, bay leaf, and 2 cups water E . Bring to a boil while stirring occasionally.

3   Reduce the heat to medium-low to maintain a simmer and cook, stirring occasionally, until the liquid reduces and thickens to the consistency of a sauce, 10 to 12 minutes F . Stir in the bacon-vegetable mixture and cook for 1 minute more to heat through. Season the chili with salt and pepper. Discard the bay leaf and thyme sprigs.

4   Spoon the chili into bowls and sprinkle each with some Gruyère and parsley. Serve hot, with a slice of toast.

SPAGHETTI *WITH CARAMELIZED LEMON, SHRIMP, AND PARSLEY*

SERVES 4

1 **lemon**

3 tablespoons extra-virgin **olive oil**

Kosher salt and **freshly ground black pepper**

2 tablespoons **unsalted butter**

12 ounces **extra-large or jumbo shrimp,** peeled and deveined

6 **garlic cloves**, thinly sliced

¼ teaspoon **crushed red pepper flakes,** plus more for garnish

½ cup **dry white wine,** such as sauvignon blanc

12 ounces **spaghetti**

¼ cup finely chopped **fresh flat-leaf parsley**

Crusty Italian bread, for serving

Allow us to rhapsodize for a moment about lemons. Unassuming as the lemon may seem, it's kind of a culinary rock star. Acidity is an essential element of cooking—it helps balance and enhance flavors—and a squeeze of lemon juice is a surefire way to add acid to any dish. In this recipe, lemons get a chance to shine two ways: as zest and in caramelized slices. Because when life gives us a lemon, we'll use the whole thing!

1 Using a Microplane, grate the zest of the lemon into a small bowl. Make sure to grate the entire surface, leaving no yellow patches behind. Cover with plastic wrap and set aside. Trim off and discard the ends of the zested lemon, then chop the lemon into ½-inch square pieces. Remove and discard any seeds.

2 Heat the olive oil in a large saucepan over medium-high heat. Add the chopped lemon, season with salt and pepper, and cook, stirring occasionally, until the lemon is caramelized in spots and the white pith is tender, 4 to 6 minutes. Transfer the lemon pieces to a bowl.

3 Add the butter to the oil left in the pot and allow it to melt. Pat the shrimp dry with a paper towel, and season with salt and pepper, then add them to the pot and cook until bright pink and just cooked through, 3 to 4 minutes, flipping them once halfway through. Using tongs, transfer the shrimp to a plate.

4 Add the garlic and red pepper flakes to the pot and cook until the garlic is lightly browned, about 1 minute. Pour in the wine and cook, scraping up the browned bits from the bottom of the pot with a wooden spoon, for about 1 minute. Add the spaghetti, 4 cups water, and a large pinch of salt. Bring the liquid to a boil, then cook, stirring every 2 minutes or so, until the spaghetti is cooked to al dente and the liquid has reduced and thickened to the consistency of a sauce, 10 to 12 minutes.

5 Stir the caramelized lemon, the lemon zest, and the parsley
into the pasta, then stir in the shrimp and season with salt
and pepper. Using tongs, pile the spaghetti and shrimp in the
center of four plates. Serve immediately, with large hunks of
crusty bread to mop up all the juices.

CREAMY CHICKEN
AND CHARRED BROCCOLI PASTA

**SERVES
4 TO 6**

4 tablespoons **olive oil**

6 cups sliced **broccoli florets** (from about 2 heads broccoli)

Kosher salt and **freshly ground black pepper**

2 tablespoons **unsalted butter**

1½ pounds boneless, skinless **chicken breasts** (about 3 breasts), cut into 1-inch cubes

1 small **yellow onion**, finely chopped

2 **garlic cloves**, minced

½ cup **dry white wine**, such as sauvignon blanc or chardonnay

3 tablespoons **all-purpose flour**

2 cups **heavy cream**

1 pound **penne** or other tubular pasta

1 cup grated **Parmesan cheese**, plus more for serving

Finely chopped **fresh flat-leaf parsley**, for serving

Let's be real: few things are more comforting than a rich, creamy pasta dish. In our version, you'll cook your pasta with the garlic, onion, and cream as well as water, so the noodles absorb those delicious flavors and add their starch to your sauce, giving it a richer consistency. Charring your broccoli before adding it lends a smoky flavor to the dish—the perfect complement to that cheesy sauce.

1 Heat 2 tablespoons of the olive oil in a large saucepan over medium-high heat. Add half the broccoli and cook, without stirring, for 2 minutes to develop a little char on the broccoli. Season with salt and pepper, then stir. Cook, stirring occasionally, until the broccoli is tender, about 3 minutes more. Using a slotted spoon, transfer the broccoli to a bowl. Repeat with the remaining 2 tablespoons of olive oil and broccoli.

2 Add the butter to the pot and swirl to evenly coat. Add the chicken, season with salt and pepper, and cook, stirring, until the chicken is golden brown in spots and cooked through, 8 to 10 minutes. Using a slotted spoon, transfer the chicken to the bowl with the broccoli.

3 Add the onion and garlic to the pot and cook, stirring occasionally, until soft and beginning to caramelize, about 3 minutes. Add the wine and cook, stirring, until it has completely evaporated, 2 to 3 minutes.

4 Sprinkle the flour evenly over the onion mixture and stir to cook the raw taste out of the flour, 2 minutes. Whisk in the cream and 4 cups water and bring to a strong simmer. Stir in the pasta and cook, stirring often, until the pasta is cooked to al dente and the liquid has reduced to the consistency of a creamy sauce, 15 minutes. Stir in the broccoli and chicken and cook for 1 minute to warm through.

5 Remove the pot from the heat and stir in the Parmesan, then season with salt and pepper. Spoon the pasta into bowls and sprinkle with more Parmesan and parsley. Serve hot.

SLOW & MULTIPURPOSE COOKERS

SLOW COOKER
TUSCAN WHITE BEAN SOUP 34

SLOW COOKER
PORK CHILI
WITH CORN BREAD 38

SLOW COOKER
CHICKEN TIKKA MASALA 39

SLOW COOKER
ASIAN-STYLE BBQ RIBS 40

MULTIPURPOSE COOKER
SHREDDED CHICKEN TACOS 43

SLOW COOKER
SPICY BUTTERNUT SQUASH SOUP
WITH PEANUT GREMOLATA 44

MULTIPURPOSE COOKER
POT ROAST
WITH MASHED CAULIFLOWER 46

MULTIPURPOSE COOKER
CREAMY CHICKPEA STEW
WITH CHILES AND CILANTRO 49

MULTIPURPOSE COOKER
CHICKEN AND RICE STEW
WITH GINGER 50

SLOW COOKER
SWORDFISH STEW
WITH TOMATOES, EGGPLANT, AND OLIVES 53

TUSCAN WHITE BEAN SOUP

Meatless Monday? Or Tuesday? Or Wednesday? Or ... okay, you get the idea—this dish is perfect for any day, especially when the weather's grim and you need the comforting goodness of a bowl of soup. Cannellini beans are a great (inexpensive) source of protein, making this a perfect veggie entrée. And if you're cooking up a big pot for meal prep, it also plays well with pasta, chicken, and (of course!) bread of all kinds.

SERVES 8

< • • • • • • • • • • • • • • >

6 cups **vegetable stock**

4 cups firmly packed coarsely chopped **kale leaves** (6 ounces)

1 teaspoon **dried oregano**

1 teaspoon **dried thyme**

4 **celery stalks**, cut into 1-inch pieces

3 medium **carrots**, cut into ¼-inch-thick rounds

3 **garlic cloves**, thinly sliced

2 (15-ounce) cans **cannellini beans**, drained and rinsed

1 (14-ounce) can diced **tomatoes**, with their juices

1 medium **white onion**, finely chopped

Kosher salt and freshly ground **black pepper**

Crusty bread, for serving

1 Combine the stock, kale, oregano, thyme, celery, carrots, garlic, beans, tomatoes with their juices, and onion in a 7-quart slow cooker. Season with at least 2 teaspoons salt and ½ teaspoon pepper. Cover and cook on High for 4 hours or Low for 8 hours.

2 Uncover and season again with salt and pepper before serving. Serve warm with a piece of crusty bread alongside.

EAT IT FOUR DIFFERENT WAYS

MAKE IT

MEAL PREP

day ①

Puree the soup and serve in bowls with Parmesan sprinkled on top.

day ②

Stir in 4 cups shredded rotisserie chicken.

Serve with a large slice of toasted sourdough bread for dipping.

Stir in 8 ounces cooked macaroni or other short pasta.

day ③

day ④

SLOW COOKER
PORK CHILI
WITH CORN BREAD

2 pounds **boneless pork shoulder**, cut into 1-inch chunks

1 tablespoon **seasoned salt**, such as Lawry's

1 tablespoon **ground cumin**

½ cup finely chopped **tomato**

½ cup finely chopped **yellow onion**

½ cup jarred **red enchilada sauce**

1 (15-ounce) can **kidney beans**, drained and rinsed

1 (8.5-ounce) box **corn bread mix**, such as Jiffy

Shredded **Cheddar cheese**, for garnish (optional)

A pork shoulder and a slow cooker are a match made in busy-chef heaven. The shoulder yields tougher meat, which benefits from a long cooking time. Why, you ask? (*puts on food science lab coat*) We're so glad you asked! Muscles mean connective tissue, which contains collagen. When it breaks down during the cooking process, collagen turns into gelatin, which transforms that tough meat into the juicy, succulent pork you know and love. Isn't science tasty?

1 Place the pork shoulder in a 7-quart slow cooker. Sprinkle the pork with the seasoned salt, cumin, tomato, and onion and pour the enchilada sauce on top. Add the beans and stir to coat the pork in the sauce and seasonings. Cover and cook on High for 3 hours.

2 Prepare the corn bread mix according to the package instructions, but do not bake the batter.

3 Uncover the slow cooker and, using a large spoon, dollop large spoonfuls of the corn bread batter evenly over the simmering chili. Cover and cook on High for 1 hour more, until the cornbread is firm and cooked through.

4 Serve the chili and corn bread in bowls, topped with Cheddar, if you like.

SLOW COOKER
CHICKEN TIKKA MASALA

2 boneless, skinless **chicken breasts**, cut into 1-inch chunks

1 tablespoon **all-purpose flour**

1 tablespoon **garam masala**

1 tablespoon **ground turmeric**

1 tablespoon **sweet paprika**

2 teaspoons **kosher salt**

½ cup canned diced **tomatoes**, with their juices

2 tablespoons **tomato paste**

4 **garlic cloves**, minced

2 **jalapeño or serrano chiles**, seeded and finely chopped

1 medium **yellow onion**, finely chopped

¾ cup **plain yogurt**

Chopped **fresh cilantro**, for garnish

Cooked **white basmati rice**, for serving

Chicken tikka masala is an Indian takeout favorite, but this slow cooker version is so easy you won't be tempted to phone it in! Garam masala is a spice rack secret weapon—it's a blend that includes cumin, coriander, cardamom, pepper, cinnamon, and cloves. Add turmeric, sweet paprika, garlic, onion, and the kick of a fresh chile, and you've got a dish that proves unforgettable flavors come in set-it-and-forget-it packages.

1   Place the chicken pieces in a 7-quart slow cooker and sprinkle with the flour, garam masala, turmeric, paprika, and salt. Stir to coat the chicken with the spices.

2   Add the canned tomatoes and their juices, tomato paste, garlic, chiles, and onion and stir to combine with the chicken.

3   Cover and cook on High for 3 hours.

4   Uncover and stir in the yogurt. Garnish the tikka masala with cilantro and serve with rice.

SLOW COOKER
ASIAN-STYLE BBQ RIBS

1 tablespoon **Chinese five-spice powder**

1 tablespoon **kosher salt**

1 tablespoon **freshly ground black pepper**

1 (2-pound) rack **spareribs**, cut in half

1 cup **chicken stock**

3 tablespoons **hoisin sauce**

1 tablespoon minced **garlic**

1 tablespoon minced **fresh ginger**

1 medium **red onion**, thinly sliced

2 teaspoons **cornstarch**

2 tablespoons **light brown sugar**

2 tablespoons **sesame seeds**

Thinly sliced **scallions** and **red chiles**, for garnish

Cooked white rice, for serving

Some food is so good, it's worth a little mess. These ribs are pure sweet, salty, a little spicy, falling-off-the-bone, finger-licking deliciousness—and while they might not be the meal you want to eat when you're wearing a white tuxedo, they are most definitely worth the odd daub of sauce on your cheek (hey, more for later!). Chinese five-spice is a blend of cinnamon, cloves, fennel, star anise, and Sichuan peppercorns, and it makes a great simple spice rub—with deliciously complex flavors.

1. On a work surface, sprinkle the five-spice powder, salt, and pepper over the ribs. Use your hands to rub the seasonings all over the ribs. Place the ribs in a 7-quart slow cooker.

2. Stir together the stock, hoisin, garlic, and ginger in a small bowl. Pour the mixture over the ribs, then scatter the onion over the top. Cover and cook on High for 3 hours or Low for 6 hours.

3. About 25 minutes before the slower cooker time is up, preheat the oven to 325°F. Line a rimmed baking sheet with foil.

4. Using tongs, carefully remove the ribs from the slow cooker and place them on the prepared baking sheet; set aside.

5. Pour the juices from the slow cooker through a strainer into a medium skillet; you should have about 1½ cups. Place the skillet over medium heat. In a small bowl, whisk together the cornstarch and ¼ cup water, then whisk the mixture into the juices in the skillet. Stir in the brown sugar and sesame seeds and cook, stirring occasionally, until the juices have reduced and thickened into a sauce, 15 to 20 minutes.

6. Using a pastry brush, brush some of the barbecue sauce on both sides of the ribs; reserve the remainder. Bake the ribs until the sauce forms a sticky glaze, about 15 minutes.

7. Separate the ribs, pile them onto a platter, and sprinkle with scallions and chiles. Serve with rice and the remaining barbecue sauce on the side.

MULTIPURPOSE COOKER
SHREDDED CHICKEN TACOS

1½ pounds boneless, skinless **chicken breasts**

1 teaspoon **chili powder**

1 teaspoon **ground cumin**

2 **garlic cloves**, minced

Kosher salt and **freshly ground black pepper**

1 (16-ounce) jar store-bought **salsa** (2 cups)

Corn or flour tortillas, **pico de gallo**, **guacamole**, and **sour cream**, for serving

Ready to give 'em something to taco 'bout? We're pretty sure anyone who tries these shredded chicken—or *tinga de pollo*—tacos won't be able to shut up about them. If you're working with a slow cooker instead of a multipurpose cooker, you can still get in on this action; just cook the chicken on low for 6 to 8 hours, or until it's cooked through. Either way, the hardest thing about this recipe is deciding which toppings to put on your finished product (might we suggest all of them?).

1 Place the chicken breasts in the multipurpose cooker. Sprinkle the chili powder, cumin, and garlic on top and season with salt and pepper. Toss until the chicken is coated with the spices. Pour the salsa over the chicken.

2 Seal the lid (you'll hear a beep when it's properly sealed) and set the pressure knob to Sealing. Select Manual and set the time to 13 minutes. It will say "On" in a few seconds. (Note: The cooker may need to warm up for 5 to 10 minutes. Steam will be released as it warms up, and a few minutes later, the time will start counting down.)

3 Once the timer goes off, using a towel or oven mitt, carefully turn the pressure knob from Sealing to Venting to release the steam in the cooker and allow the pressure to come down naturally, 20 to 25 minutes. After all the steam has been released, release the lid and use two forks to shred the chicken and mix it evenly with the salsa.

4 Serve the chicken in tortillas, topped with pico de gallo, guacamole, and sour cream.

SLOW COOKER
SPICY BUTTERNUT SQUASH SOUP
WITH PEANUT GREMOLATA

SOUP

2¼ pounds **butternut squash**, peeled and and cut into 1-inch cubes (about 7 cups)

2 **garlic cloves**

1 medium **yellow onion**, coarsely chopped

1 (15-ounce) can whole peeled **tomatoes**, with their juices

1 **Scotch bonnet or habanero chile**, stemmed, seeded, and coarsely chopped

4 cups low-sodium **chicken stock**

Kosher salt and **freshly ground black pepper**

Freshly grated **nutmeg**

PEANUT GREMOLATA

¼ cup **olive oil**

2 cups **bread crumbs** (4 ounces), preferably made from stale **sourdough bread**

½ cup **unsalted peanuts**, chopped

Finely grated **zest of 1 lemon**

1 cup lightly packed **fresh cilantro** leaves, coarsely chopped

Kosher salt and **freshly ground black pepper**

Gremolata is a classic Italian condiment used as a garnish for all kinds of dishes (it's especially good for adding some brightness to heavy meats). Ours is a twist on the traditional version, which is made with parsley, garlic, and lemon zest. The addition of bread crumbs and peanuts give this version a nice crunch, perfect for adding a little texture to the smooth soup. We love the combination of cilantro with the soup's heat, but for all you cilantro haters out there, feel free to swap in parsley.

1 Make the soup: Combine the squash, garlic, onion, tomatoes and their juices, and chile in a slow cooker. Pour in the stock, season with salt and pepper, and stir to combine. Cover and cook on High for 3 hours or Low for 6 hours.

2 While the soup cooks, make the gremolata: Heat the olive oil in a large skillet over medium heat. Add the bread crumbs and cook, stirring, until starting to brown, 6 to 8 minutes. Add the peanuts and cook, stirring and tossing, until the bread crumbs are crisp and brown and the nuts are toasted, 3 to 5 minutes. Transfer the bread crumbs and nuts to a bowl and immediately stir in the lemon zest. Let the mixture cool, then stir in the cilantro and season with salt and pepper.

3 Uncover the slow cooker and, using an immersion blender (or working in batches with a regular blender), puree the soup until smooth. Season the soup with salt, pepper, and nutmeg.

4 Ladle the soup into bowls and sprinkle with the gremolata before serving.

MULTIPURPOSE COOKER
POT ROAST
WITH MASHED CAULIFLOWER

POT ROAST

1 (1½-pound) **boneless beef chuck roast**

Kosher salt and **freshly ground black pepper**

1 tablespoon **vegetable oil**

2 cups **beef stock**

4 medium **carrots**, cut into 2-inch lengths

2 **garlic cloves**, minced

1 large **white onion**, thinly sliced

2 tablespoons **all-purpose flour**

1 tablespoon **unsalted butter**, at room temperature

MASHED CAULIFLOWER

1 (2½-pound) head **cauliflower**, cored and broken into florets

1 cup **beef stock**

Kosher salt and **freshly ground black pepper**

1 tablespoon **sour cream**

1 **garlic clove**, minced

Finely chopped **fresh chives**, for garnish

Sometimes, a little pressure is a good thing—like when it's a song by David Bowie and Queen, or when it comes to cooking pot roast. If you've never used the pressure function on your multi-cooker before, don't worry—we'll walk you through it! Just remember to protect your hands with a kitchen towel or oven mitt when you release the pressure knob, because things tend to get a little steamy in there while the magic is happening. Okay, maybe it's not actually magic, but melt-in-your-mouth pot roast that cooks this fast and cauliflower that tastes this creamy? That's a pretty neat trick.

1. Make the pot roast: On a work surface, pat the roast dry with paper towels. Season with salt and pepper on all sides.

2. Set the multipurpose cooker to Sauté. Once it says "Hot," add the vegetable oil. Add the roast and cook, turning as needed, until the meat is seared all over, including on the ends, and golden brown, 3 to 5 minutes per side. Add the stock, carrots, garlic, and onion and stir until the vegetables are evenly distributed.

3. Seal the lid (you'll hear a beep when it's properly sealed) and set the pressure knob to Sealing. Select Manual and set the time to 50 minutes. It will say "On" in a few seconds. (Note: The cooker may need to warm up for 5 to 10 minutes. Steam will be released as it warms up, and a few minutes later, the time will start counting down.) After the time has expired, let the pot roast rest in the pot for 10 minutes. It will count up and read "L 0:10" on the screen.

4   Using a towel or oven mitt, carefully turn the pressure knob from Sealing to Venting to release the steam in the cooker and allow the pressure to come down naturally, 20 to 25 minutes. After all the steam has been released, release the lid and use tongs to carefully transfer the roast and vegetables to a plate or cutting board, leaving the liquid in the pot. Cover the roast and vegetables with foil to keep warm.

5   Set the cooker to Sauté and allow the liquid in the pot to come to a boil. Meanwhile, mash together the flour and butter in a small bowl until they form a thick paste. Spoon 3 tablespoons of the liquid in the pot into the flour-butter mixture and stir until completely smooth. Add the slurry to the liquid in the pot and whisk until the liquid thickens to the consistency of a sauce, 1 to 2 minutes. Hit Cancel and remove the pot from the cooker. Pour the sauce through a strainer into a small bowl and cover to keep warm. Clean out the pot and return it to the cooker.

6   Make the mashed cauliflower: Place the cauliflower florets in the pot and pour in the stock. Season with salt and pepper. Seal the lid (you'll hear a beep when it's properly sealed) and set the pressure knob to Sealing. Select Manual and set the time to 5 minutes. Once the time is up, using a towel or an oven mitt, carefully turn the pressure knob from Sealing to Venting to release the steam in the cooker and allow the pressure to come down naturally, 20 to 25 minutes. After all the steam has been released, release the lid, carefully remove the pot, and drain the cauliflower in a colander.

7   Return the cauliflower to the pot and, using a potato masher or fork, mash the cauliflower until smooth. Stir in the sour cream and garlic and season again with salt and pepper.

8   Top the mashed cauliflower with chives and serve alongside the pot roast, vegetables, and gravy.

MULTIPURPOSE COOKER
CREAMY CHICKPEA STEW
WITH CHILES AND CILANTRO

SERVES 6

2 cups **dried chickpeas**

¼ cup **olive oil**

1 tablespoon **ground cumin**

10 **garlic cloves**

2 medium **yellow onions**, halved lengthwise

2 small **carrots**, halved lengthwise

2 **serrano chiles**, stemmed and seeded

1 large bunch **fresh cilantro**, stems and leaves separated

Kosher salt and **freshly ground black pepper**

Plain Greek yogurt, for serving

Budget-friendly? Check. Vegetarian? Check. (Vegan if you skip the yogurt!) Protein-packed garlicky goodness? Big ol' check. Yup, this recipe checks a lot of boxes. We could write sonnets about our love of chickpeas (*How do we love 'peas? Let us count the ways . . .*), and one of our favorite things about them is how creamy they are when blended—no dairy required. Who knew comfort food could be this healthy?

1 Place the chickpeas in the multipurpose cooker, then top with the olive oil, cumin, garlic, onions, carrots, chiles, cilantro stems, 2 teaspoons salt, and 6 cups water.

2 Seal the lid (you'll hear a beep when it's properly sealed) and set the pressure knob to Sealing. Select Manual and set the time to 40 minutes. It will say "On" in a few seconds. (Note: The cooker may need to warm up for 5 to 10 minutes. Steam will be released as it warms up, and a few minutes later, the time will start counting down.)

3 Once the timer goes off, using a towel or oven mitt, turn the pressure knob from Sealing to Venting to release the steam in the cooker and allow the pressure to come down naturally, 20 to 25 minutes. After all the steam has been released, release the lid and use a slotted spoon to transfer half the chickpeas (about 1½ cups) to a bowl.

4 Using an immersion blender (or working in batches in a regular blender), puree the ingredients remaining in the cooker until smooth. Stir in the reserved whole chickpeas and half the cilantro leaves and season with salt and pepper.

5 Spoon the soup into bowls. Top each with a dollop of yogurt and swirl it into the top. Sprinkle with the remaining cilantro and serve hot.

MULTIPURPOSE COOKER
CHICKEN AND RICE STEW
WITH GINGER

SERVES 4

1 (3- to 4-pound) **whole chicken**

2 **scallions**, halved crosswise, plus thinly sliced scallion for garnish

1 (5-inch) piece **fresh ginger**, peeled and halved

¾ cup **jasmine rice**, rinsed well

1 tablespoon **toasted sesame oil**, plus more for serving

1 tablespoon **kosher salt**

Freshly ground black pepper

Toasted sesame seeds and **soy sauce**, for serving

Separately, chicken soup and ginger are both popular remedies for the common cold. This stew brings them together into what might just be a *super-remedy* . . . okay, it might not actually cure your cold, but we can pretty much guarantee you'll feel better after eating it (whether you're sick or not). Oh, and hot ginger tip: You can use the side of a spoon to peel it!

1   Place the chicken in the multipurpose cooker, then top with the scallion halves, ginger, rice, sesame oil, salt, and 6 cups water A .

2   Seal the lid (you'll hear a beep when it's properly sealed) and set the pressure knob to Sealing. Select Manual and set the time to 20 minutes B . It will say "On" in a few seconds. (Note: The cooker may need to warm up for 5 to 10 minutes. Steam will be released as it warms up, and a few minutes later, the time will start counting down.)

3   Once the timer goes off, using a towel or oven mitt, carefully turn the pressure knob to Quick Release to rapidly release the steam in the cooker and bring the pressure down quickly, 1 to 2 minutes C . After all the steam has been released, release the lid and use tongs to transfer the chicken to a bowl. Pick off and discard the skin and bones and shred the meat with two forks D . Return the meat to the pot and stir to combine.

4   Season the stew with pepper and spoon into bowls. Serve with sliced scallions, sesame oil, sesame seeds, and soy sauce for topping the stew as you like.

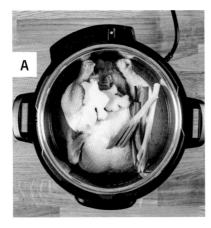

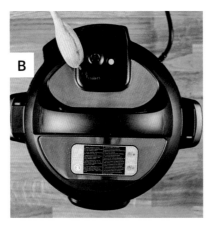

SLOW COOKER
SWORDFISH STEW
WITH TOMATOES, EGGPLANT, AND OLIVES

¼ cup **extra-virgin olive oil**, plus more for serving

½ teaspoon **crushed red pepper flakes**

3 **garlic cloves**, finely chopped

2 (28-ounce) cans whole peeled **tomatoes**, with their juices, crushed by hand

1 large **eggplant** (about 1½ pounds), trimmed and cut into ½-inch cubes

1 cup **vegetable stock** or water

Kosher salt and **freshly ground black pepper**

4 (1-inch-thick) skinless **swordfish steaks**, about 6 ounces each

1 cup large **green olives**, pitted and coarsely chopped

¼ cup **capers**, drained and rinsed

¼ cup coarsely chopped **fresh flat-leaf parsley**, plus more for serving

1 tablespoon **fresh lemon juice**

Crusty bread or **cooked polenta**, for serving

Even if you've never cooked with swordfish, we think you should take a stab at this dish. (Get it?) In contrast with more delicate white-fleshed fish like tilapia, swordfish is more like a sea-steak: meaty and substantial. It's got a strong flavor, which means it won't be overwhelmed by the briny capers and olives, acidic tomatoes, and spicy red pepper flakes in this stew. When it comes to bold taste, this one slays.

1 Combine the olive oil, red pepper flakes, garlic, tomatoes and their juices, eggplant, and stock in a 7-quart slow cooker. Season with salt and pepper and stir to combine. Cover and cook on High for 3 hours or Low for 6 hours.

2 Season the swordfish steaks all over with salt and pepper. Uncover the slow cooker and submerge the steaks in the tomato-eggplant sauce. Sprinkle the olives and capers over the top of the sauce. Cover and cook on High for 30 minutes, until the swordfish is just cooked through.

3 Lift the steaks out of the sauce with a spoon and transfer each to an individual serving bowl. Stir the parsley and lemon juice into the sauce, then spoon the sauce over each steak. Sprinkle with more parsley and drizzle with more olive oil. Serve with crusty bread or over polenta.

DIENTS
(OR FEWER)

CHILI-GLAZED SALMON

Once you have a jar of Asian sweet chili sauce in your fridge, we defy you not to eat it with *everything*. You'll forgive us that mild hyperbole once you try this sweet-and-spicy mixture of chiles, vinegar, sugar, and garlic. It makes a perfect dip for everything from french fries to egg rolls and, as in this recipe, an excellent one-step marinade. The sauce will caramelize as it bakes, creating a delicious crust on top of the fish. (And if you want to spoon a little extra over your veggies, we totally support you.)

‹••••••••••••••›

4 (4-ounce) skin-on **salmon fillets**

Kosher salt and **freshly ground black pepper**

⅔ cup **Asian sweet chili sauce**

⅓ cup finely chopped **scallions**

Cooked **broccoli florets** or **sugar snap peas**, for serving

1 Preheat the oven to 400°F. Line a baking sheet with parchment paper or foil.

2 Place the salmon fillets on the prepared baking sheet, skin-side down. Season with salt and pepper.

3 Stir together the chili sauce and scallions in a small bowl. Spoon the sauce over the salmon fillets, coating them completely. Bake until the salmon is just cooked through, 12 to 15 minutes for medium doneness.

4 Using a metal spatula, transfer the fillets to individual plates, leaving the skin behind on the baking sheet, and serve with broccoli or sugar snap peas.

EAT IT FOUR DIFFERENT WAYS

MAKE IT

MEAL PREP

day ①

Serve with steamed broccoli on the side.

day ②

Break up into bite-size pieces and stir into fried rice.

Finely chop and use to make sushi rolls with cooked rice and sheets of nori.

Serve with a side of shredded cabbage and carrots dressed with rice vinegar and toasted sesame oil.

day ③

day ④

CAULIFLOWER MAC 'N' CHEESE

1 (2½-pound) head **cauliflower**, cored and broken into florets (about 5 cups)

½ cup **sour cream** or **plain Greek yogurt**

1 cup shredded **Cheddar cheese** (4 ounces)

Kosher salt and **freshly ground black pepper**

Finely chopped **fresh flat-leaf parsley**, for garnish (optional)

Salad greens, for serving

Culinarily, is there anything cauliflower can't do? It can be a pizza crust, a creamy mash, fried "rice," and now a delicious low-carb substitute for macaroni. Because look, we love carbs as much as anyone (actually, probably more than most people—perhaps you're familiar with our work with desserts?), but sometimes you want to avoid a carbo-load. With apologies to our dear friend, pasta, this dish is so good, you don't even miss the mac. Oh, and it's the perfect way to sneak some veggies onto a picky eater's plate.

1 Bring a large pot of water to a boil over high heat. Add the cauliflower and cook until just tender, about 5 minutes. Drain the cauliflower in a colander, then return it to the pot.

2 Place the pot over low heat and stir in the sour cream. Add the Cheddar and stir until it has melted. Season the cauliflower mac 'n' cheese with salt and pepper.

3 Remove the pot from the heat and divide the mac 'n' cheese among four serving plates. Sprinkle with parsley, if you like, and serve with salad on the side.

BBQ CHICKEN–STUFFED SWEET POTATOES

SERVES 4

2 large **sweet potatoes**

2 tablespoons **olive oil**

Kosher salt and **freshly ground black pepper**

2 cups shredded **red cabbage** (5 ounces)

⅔ cup **barbecue sauce**, plus more for serving

2 cooked **chicken breasts** (from a rotisserie chicken), bones removed, finely chopped

¼ cup thinly sliced **scallions**

You'll never hear us hating on a half-homemade meal. Being an adult is hard (we have to wash dishes *every single time* we use them?), so we say take advantage of whatever hacks you can. Speaking of which, a store-bought rotisserie chicken is a great hack, both for this recipe and for meal prep generally. You'll only need the breasts for these stuffed sweet potatoes, so you can use the rest for another recipe. (Might we suggest the Chicken, Broccoli, and Cheddar Pockets on page 160?)

1 Preheat the oven to 425°F. Line a baking sheet with parchment paper or foil.

2 Place the sweet potatoes on the prepared baking sheet and prick them all over with a fork. Rub them all over with the olive oil, then season with salt and pepper. Bake until the sweet potatoes are tender in the center when pierced with a paring knife, 40 to 50 minutes. Remove the sweet potatoes from the oven and let cool for 10 minutes.

3 Combine the cabbage and barbecue sauce in a medium skillet. Cook over medium heat, stirring, until the cabbage starts to soften, about 3 minutes A . Stir in the chopped chicken B , then remove the skillet from the heat and season the mixture with salt and pepper C .

4 Once the sweet potatoes are cool enough to handle, slice each in half lengthwise and scoop out their flesh with a spoon, leaving a ¼-inch-thick layer attached to the skins D . Transfer the flesh to a bowl and mash with a fork until smooth. Season with salt and pepper and set aside.

5 Fill the sweet potato shells with the chicken-cabbage filling E , drizzle with more barbecue sauce, and top with the scallions. Serve with mashed sweet potatoes on the side.

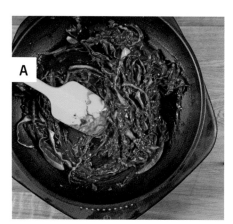

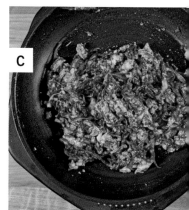

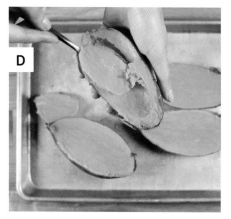

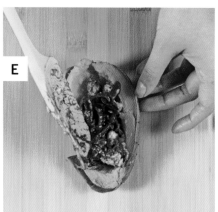

FLANK STEAK
WITH MUSTARDY ONIONS AND ROSEMARY

1 tablespoon **olive oil**

1 (1¾-pound) **flank steak**, halved crosswise

Kosher salt and **freshly ground black pepper**

1 small **yellow onion**, thinly sliced lengthwise

1 **garlic clove**, minced

Leaves from 1 small sprig **fresh rosemary**, minced, plus more for garnish

2 tablespoons **Dijon mustard**

Cooked potatoes or **pasta**, for serving

Caramelizing onions is one of those chef skills you'll whip out again and again. Once you're comfortable with the technique, you'll find all kinds of different uses for these little sweet-yet-savory miracles. Pizza topping? Duh. Burger garnish? Oh, yeah. Scrambled egg accent? Now you're talking! The technique itself is simple: just stir your onions frequently—you don't want them to brown too much in any one place; you want them a uniform golden brown.

1 Heat the olive oil in a large skillet over medium-high heat. Season the steaks all over with salt and pepper, then add them to the skillet and cook, undisturbed, until browned on the bottom, 5 to 6 minutes. Flip the steaks and cook for 4 minutes for medium-rare doneness. Transfer the steaks to a plate.

2 Return the skillet to medium heat and add the onion, garlic, and rosemary. Cook, stirring to scrape up any browned bits from the bottom of the pan, until the onion is soft and caramelized, about 6 minutes. Stir in the mustard and ½ cup water, bring to a simmer, and cook until the sauce thickens, 3 to 4 minutes. Remove the skillet from the heat and season with salt and pepper.

3 Thinly slice the steak and divide it among four plates. Spoon the mustard-onion sauce over the steak and sprinkle with more rosemary to garnish. Serve with potatoes or pasta alongside.

EASY RAVIOLI "LASAGNA"

Olive oil, for greasing
1½ pounds **cheese ravioli**
3 cups **tomato-meat sauce**
2 cups shredded **mozzarella cheese** (8 ounces)
Salad greens, for serving (optional)

We at Tasty loooove a good shortcut. And a shortcut that involves double cheese? We'd call that pretty great—or even … grate? Puns aside, this dish is the perfect stupid-simple go-to for busy weeknights. By swapping out lasagna noodles for store-bought ravioli, not only do you lose a step (no need to boil the pasta), but you gain an extra layer of cheesy goodness.

1   Preheat the oven to 400°F. Line a baking sheet with foil. Grease a 2½- to 3-quart baking dish with olive oil and set it on the lined baking sheet.

2   Spread half the ravioli in an even layer over the bottom of the prepared baking dish A , then spoon over half the tomato-meat sauce B . Sprinkle the sauce evenly with half the cheese C . Top with the remaining ravioli in an even layer, then cover with the remaining sauce D . Sprinkle the remaining cheese on top E . When all the layers are complete F , cover the dish with foil.

3   Bake for 30 minutes, then remove the foil and continue baking until the "lasagna" is bubbling in the center and the cheese is golden brown on top, about 10 minutes more.

4   Let the lasagna cool for 10 minutes, then serve with salad alongside, if you like.

SALSA-BRAISED CHICKEN

SERVES 4

WITH AVOCADO

8 bone-in, skin-on **chicken thighs** (3 pounds)

Kosher salt and **freshly ground black pepper**

3 cups **salsa verde**

½ cup **white wine**

2 ripe **avocados**, pitted, peeled, and cubed

¼ cup finely chopped **fresh cilantro** leaves

Warmed tortillas, for serving (optional)

We want to talk about something very close to our hearts: pan sauce. Making pan sauce ensures you don't waste any of the rendered fat from the meat you're cooking *and* makes that meat taste so much more flavorful. In this recipe, you'll deglaze (fancy chef word for stirring up all the tasty browned bits) your pan with white wine, then add salsa to create a braising sauce that will lend flavor and tenderness to your chicken as it continues to cook. Our motto: Waste not (fat), want not (flavor).

1   Preheat the oven to 400°F.

2   Season the chicken thighs all over with salt and pepper and place them skin-side down in a large, cold ovenproof skillet. Place the skillet over medium-high heat and cook the chicken thighs, undisturbed, until the skin is golden brown and the thighs naturally release from the skillet, about 5 minutes. Using tongs, transfer the thighs to paper towels.

3   Stir the salsa and wine into the rendered fat in the skillet, then remove the skillet from the heat. Return the thighs to the skillet, skin-side up, so they are half submerged in the sauce. Transfer the skillet to the oven and bake until the chicken is cooked through and tender and the sauce has reduced and thickened, about 30 minutes.

4   Remove the skillet from the oven, scatter the avocado pieces evenly around the chicken in the sauce, and let the chicken rest in the sauce for 10 minutes.

5   Sprinkle the chicken, avocados, and sauce with the cilantro, and serve with tortillas on the side, if desired.

SPICY RICE NOODLES

WITH GROUND PORK AND SCALLIONS

14 ounces wide flat **rice noodles**, such as for pad thai

2 tablespoons **toasted sesame oil**, plus more for serving

1½ pounds **ground pork**

6 **scallions**, white and light green parts minced, dark green parts thinly sliced

Kosher salt and **freshly ground black pepper**

2 tablespoons **chile-garlic paste**, plus more for serving

Rice noodles are a staple of Thai and Vietnamese cuisine (if you've ever eaten pad thai, you're familiar with their charms). They're just as easy to cook as wheat pasta (plus, they're gluten-free!) but require a slightly different technique: instead of cooking them in still-boiling water, boil the water first and add it to your noodles off the heat. They're more delicate than wheat noodles, and cooking them off the stove ensures that they don't get mushy. Crispy pork, nutty sesame oil, and spicy chile-garlic paste make this noodle dish a slam-dunk for anyone who loves the flavors of Asian cuisines.

1 Place the noodles in a large bowl and add boiling water to cover. Let stand for 5 minutes to soften.

2 While the noodles are soaking, heat the sesame oil in a wok or large skillet over high heat. Add the pork and minced scallions, season with salt and pepper, and cook, stirring, until browned, 6 to 8 minutes.

3 Reserve ¼ cup of the noodle soaking water and drain the noodles. Add the noodles, reserved soaking water, and the chile-garlic paste to the wok and cook, stirring continuously, until the noodles are evenly coated in the sauce.

4 Transfer the noodles and sauce to serving bowls and top with the sliced scallion greens. Serve with more sesame oil and chile-garlic paste on the side.

STIR-FRIED BELL PEPPERS
WITH SHRIMP AND GARLIC

SERVES 4

3 tablespoons **olive oil**

1½ pounds **jumbo shrimp**, peeled (tails left on) and deveined

Kosher salt and **freshly ground black pepper**

3 medium **bell peppers** (preferably a mix of red and yellow or orange, no green), thinly sliced lengthwise

4 **garlic cloves**, very thinly sliced

1½ teaspoons **smoked paprika**

2 tablespoons finely chopped **fresh flat-leaf parsley**

Cooked rice or **crusty bread**, for serving

Every home chef needs a good stir-fry in their arsenal—it's quick, easy, and wildly versatile. We love the combination of shrimp and bell peppers, but if you want to up the veggie content, broccoli, asparagus, or snow peas would be great additions, if you happen to have them in your fridge.

1 Heat 2 tablespoons of the olive oil in a large skillet over medium-high heat. Season the shrimp all over with salt and black pepper, then add them to the skillet in a single layer. Cook, undisturbed, until golden brown on the bottom, about 2 minutes. Flip the shrimp and cook until just cooked through, about 2 minutes more. Using tongs, transfer the shrimp to a plate.

2 Return the skillet to medium-high heat and pour in the remaining 1 tablespoon olive oil. Add the bell peppers and garlic, season with salt and black pepper, and cook, stirring occasionally, until the peppers are tender and caramelized, 5 to 7 minutes. Sprinkle with the paprika and cook, stirring, until fragrant, about 1 minute more.

3 Divide the peppers and shrimp among four plates, top with the parsley, and serve with cooked rice or crusty bread.

20 MINUTES

(TOPS)

ZUCCHINI PARMESAN
FRITTERS

Realistically, we should all be eating more vegetables. But you know what they say: the road to late-night sour-cream-and-onion chips is paved with good intentions. Enter: these fritters. With a full pound of zucchini, they give you the veggies you need. Besides being sneakily healthy, the fritters are a great addition to your meal-prep arsenal—not only do they make a perfect complement to fish and noodles, they're also shaped like mini breads, which can only mean one thing: Tiny. Sandwiches. Go ahead— fritter your days away.

SERVES 4

‹• • • • • • • • • • • • • • •›

1 pound **zucchini**, trimmed and finely chopped (3 cups)

½ cup grated **Parmesan cheese**

½ cup **all-purpose flour**

2 tablespoons **fresh lemon juice**

3 **garlic cloves**, minced

1 large **egg**

Kosher salt and **freshly ground black pepper**

2 tablespoons **vegetable oil**, plus more as needed

Sour cream and **salad greens** or **mashed potatoes**, for serving

1 Bring 2 cups water to a boil in a large saucepan. Add the zucchini and cook, stirring, until slightly tender, about 3 minutes. Drain the zucchini in a colander and let cool for 5 minutes.

2 Transfer the zucchini to a large bowl and stir in the Parmesan, flour, lemon juice, garlic, and egg. Season with salt and pepper and stir to combine.

3 Heat the vegetable oil in a large skillet over medium-high heat. Working in batches, use a spoon to drop heaping tablespoons of the zucchini batter into the skillet. Flatten them slightly to form fritters and cook until the fritters are golden brown and crisp, about 4 minutes, flipping them once halfway through. Transfer the fritters to paper towels to drain and sprinkle with more salt. Repeat with the remaining batter, adding more oil to the skillet between batches, if necessary.

4 Divide the fritters among four plates and serve with sour cream and a salad or mashed potatoes.

EAT IT FOUR DIFFERENT WAYS

MAKE IT

MEAL
PREP

day ①

Serve with a cooked skinless fillet of cod or other firm, white-fleshed fish.

day ②

Serve with a side of buttered cooked egg noodles sprinkled with Parmesan.

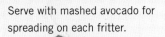

Serve with mashed avocado for spreading on each fritter.

Place smoked salmon, sliced red onion, and a dollop of sour cream between two fritters to make mini sandwiches.

day ③

day ④

CHEESY CHICKEN AND BEAN SKILLET BAKE

SERVES 4 TO 6

2 tablespoons **vegetable oil**

2½ pounds boneless, skinless **chicken breasts**, cut into ½-inch pieces

Kosher salt and **freshly ground black pepper**

1 small **white onion**, minced

2 **garlic cloves**, minced

2 tablespoons **chili powder**

1 tablespoon **all-purpose flour**

2 teaspoons **ground coriander**

1 teaspoon **ground cumin**

2 (15-ounce) cans **pinto or pink beans**, drained and rinsed

2 (10-ounce) cans diced **tomatoes with chiles**, such as Ro-Tel

3 cups shredded **Monterey or pepper Jack cheese** (12 ounces)

Fresh cilantro leaves, for garnish (optional)

Quick, hearty, and one-skillet? Yeah, this dish hits the weeknight dinner trifecta. Speaking of power trios, let's talk about coriander, cumin, and chili powder, the spices that lend complexity to the flavors of this dish. Coriander and cumin are a classic duo, ubiquitous in South Asian and Latin American cuisine. They add an earthy, citrusy flavor to dishes, which plays perfectly with the spicy kick of chili powder.

1 Preheat the oven to 425°F.

2 Heat the vegetable oil in a large ovenproof skillet over medium-high heat. Season the chicken with salt and pepper, then add to the skillet and cook, stirring, until no longer pink, about 5 minutes. Add the onion and garlic and cook, stirring, until the onion is softened and the chicken is cooked through, about 5 minutes more. Stir in the chili powder, flour, coriander, and cumin.

3 Remove the skillet from the heat and stir in the beans and tomatoes with chiles. Top evenly with the shredded cheese, then transfer the skillet to the oven and bake until the mixture is bubbling in the center and the cheese is melted and browned on top, about 10 minutes.

4 Remove the skillet from the oven and garnish with cilantro, if you like, before serving.

BEEF AND BROCCOLI NOODLE STIR-FRY

SERVES 4

3 (3-ounce) packages **instant ramen**, seasoning packets discarded or reserved for another use

⅓ cup **soy sauce**

2 tablespoons **toasted sesame oil**

2 tablespoons **fresh lime juice**

1 teaspoon **cornstarch**

½ teaspoon **kosher salt**

3 teaspoons **olive oil**

12 ounces **flank steak**, thinly sliced

1 medium **yellow onion**, thinly sliced

1 **garlic clove**, minced

2 cups **broccoli florets**

2 tablespoons thinly sliced **scallions**

2 tablespoons finely chopped **fresh cilantro**

1½ teaspoons toasted **sesame seeds**

In the US, ramen has recently started to come out from under a reputation as the exclusive purview of broke students. And it's about time, because it turns out, instant ramen—while insubstantial, albeit delicious, on its own—is a great addition to stir-fries. Another major time-saver? Microwaving your broccoli so it will cook more quickly in your skillet. No shame in that microwave game!

1 Place the ramen noodles in a large bowl and pour 8 cups boiling water over the top. Let the noodles sit, stirring them every now and then to break up the noodle blocks, until just tender, 4 to 6 minutes. Drain the noodles and rinse under cold water. Return the noodles to the bowl and cover with plastic wrap to keep them moist.

2 While the noodles soak, stir together the soy sauce, sesame oil, lime juice, cornstarch, and salt in a small bowl.

3 Heat 1 teaspoon of the olive oil in a large nonstick skillet over high heat. Add the steak to the pan, drizzle with 2 tablespoons of the sauce, and cook, tossing, until browned, about 2 minutes. Transfer the steak to a bowl.

4 Add 1 teaspoon of the olive oil to the skillet, then add the onion and garlic and cook, stirring often, until soft and browned, about 4 minutes. Meanwhile, place the broccoli in a large, microwave-safe bowl and microwave until soft, about 2 minutes. Add the broccoli to the skillet and cook, stirring, until lightly browned and crisped, about 2 minutes. Transfer the onion and broccoli to the bowl with the steak.

5 Add the remaining 1 teaspoon olive oil to the skillet, then add the noodles and the remaining sauce and cook, stirring continuously, until the noodles have soaked up the sauce. Return the cooked vegetables and steak to the skillet and toss to combine. Transfer the noodles to a serving dish and sprinkle with the scallions, cilantro, and sesame seeds before serving.

VEGAN FETTUCCINE ALFREDO

2 teaspoons **kosher salt**, plus more as needed

1 pound **fettuccine pasta**

¼ cup **olive oil**

¼ cup **all-purpose flour**

2 cups **unsweetened almond milk** or other nut milk

2 cups **raw cashews** (11 ounces)

¼ cup **nutritional yeast**

2 tablespoons **fresh lemon juice**

1 teaspoon **onion powder**

1 teaspoon **garlic powder**

¼ teaspoon **freshly ground black pepper**

1 **garlic clove**, coarsely chopped

Finely chopped **fresh flat-leaf parsley**, for garnish (optional)

Fettuccine Alfredo has a reputation for being richer than a Rockefeller and more dairy-filled than Wisconsin, but we love a challenge—so we decided to give it a vegan overhaul. Cashews and nut milk give this sauce the creaminess of traditional Alfredo. (Make sure you choose an unsweetened, unflavored nut milk!) For the uninitiated, nutritional yeast is a deactivated yeast (meaning it won't make bread rise) that has an umami, cheesy flavor. You don't have to be a vegan to fall in love with this dreamy sauce!

1 Bring a large pot of salted water to a boil. Add the fettuccine and cook, stirring occasionally, until cooked to al dente, about 10 minutes.

2 While the pasta cooks, heat the olive oil in a large saucepan over medium heat. Add the flour and cook, stirring often, to cook out the raw flour taste, about 1 minute. Pour in the almond milk and cook, whisking continuously, until the liquid comes to a boil and thickens. Remove the pan from the heat.

3 In a blender, combine the 2 teaspoons salt, cashews, nutritional yeast, lemon juice, onion powder, garlic powder, pepper, and chopped garlic. Turn the blender on and slowly pour the hot almond milk sauce into the blender. Blend until the mixture is smooth. If necessary, pour in up to ½ cup of the pasta cooking water to help the sauce puree smoothly. Pour the sauce back into the pan and bring to a simmer over medium heat.

4 Once the pasta is cooked, reserve 2 cups of the cooking water and drain the pasta. Add the pasta and reserved cooking water to the Alfredo sauce and toss to coat. Divide the pasta among four bowls and top with chopped parsley, if you like, before serving.

MEDITERRANEAN FLATBREAD

1½ tablespoons **olive oil**

8 cups chopped **kale leaves** (8 ounces)

Kosher salt

¼ cup **pine nuts**

4 **garlic cloves**, minced

Crushed red pepper flakes

⅔ cup thinly sliced **sun-dried tomatoes in oil**, drained, plus 4 teaspoons oil from the jar

Freshly ground black pepper

4 store-bought **flatbreads** or **pocketless pitas**

¾ cup **hummus**

When your brain is saying "Pizza!" and your body's saying "Please ... vitamins ...," this flatbread is the perfect compromise. Thanks to the protein-rich hummus and pine nuts, it's substantial enough for a main course, but it's also the perfect party appetizer for projecting "I am succeeding at adulthood!"

1 Heat 1 tablespoon of the olive oil in a large skillet over medium heat. Add the kale, season with salt, and cook, stirring, until half wilted, about 4 minutes. Add 1 tablespoon water and cook until the kale is fully wilted, about 4 minutes more.

2 Push the kale to the perimeter of the skillet and pour the remaining ½ tablespoon olive oil into the center of the skillet. Add the pine nuts, garlic, and red pepper flakes to the oil and cook, stirring, until the garlic is fragrant and the pine nuts are toasted, about 2 minutes. Add the sun-dried tomatoes and cook, stirring to combine with the kale and aromatics, until the kale is fully wilted, about 3 minutes more. Remove the skillet from the heat and season with salt and black pepper.

3 While the kale is cooking, preheat the broiler to high.

4 Place the flatbreads on a baking sheet and brush each with 1 teaspoon of the oil from the jar of sun-dried tomatoes. Broil, flipping halfway through, until golden brown and toasted on both sides, about 4 minutes.

5 Transfer the flatbreads to a cutting board and spread 3 tablespoons of the hummus over each. Divide the kale mixture among the flatbreads, cut each into 4 pieces, and serve.

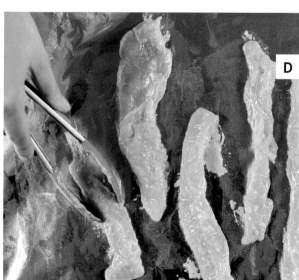

CHICKEN TENDERS AND CABBAGE SLAW
WITH MISO-LIME DRESSING

SERVES 4

½ cup **vegetable oil**

¼ cup plus 2 tablespoons **fresh lime juice**

4 tablespoons **white miso**

1 teaspoon finely grated **fresh ginger**

¼ teaspoon **sugar**

1½ pounds boneless, skinless **chicken breasts**, cut lengthwise into ½-inch-thick tenders

Kosher salt and **freshly ground black pepper**

4 medium **carrots**, shredded

3 large **scallions**, white and light green parts only, very thinly sliced lengthwise

1 small **green cabbage**, shredded (8 cups)

½ cup lightly packed **fresh cilantro leaves**

No shade to miso soup, but if that's the only way you've eaten the umami-packed wonder paste that is miso, you're leaving a lot of flavor on the table. Miso is a paste made from soybeans fermented with a grain—rice, in the case of white miso. It's very salty, kind of funky, and perfect in marinades and dressings. In this recipe, you'll combine it with lime juice, ginger, and sugar to create a dressing for your cabbage slaw and an extra flavor coating on those chicken tenders (what a multitasker)! We suspect that after this meal, you'll be a convert to the church of miso, so here's some more good news: it'll last for about nine months in your fridge. We have a hunch that you and miso *ferment* to be.

1 In a small bowl, whisk together the vegetable oil, ¼ cup of the lime juice, 3 tablespoons of the miso, the ginger, and the sugar to create the dressing A . Pour ½ cup of the dressing into a large bowl, mix in the remaining 1 tablespoon miso, and add the chicken B . Season the chicken with salt and pepper and toss until fully coated with dressing.

2 To make the slaw, whisk the remaining 2 tablespoons lime juice into the remaining dressing, then add the carrots, scallions, and cabbage C . Season with salt and pepper and toss to combine. Cover the slaw with plastic wrap and refrigerate while you cook the chicken.

3 Preheat the broiler to high. Line a baking sheet with foil. Arrange the chicken on the baking sheet and season with more salt and pepper D . Broil until cooked through and caramelized on top, about 6 minutes, flipping once halfway through E . Remove the baking sheet from the broiler.

4 Stir the cilantro into the slaw, then divide it among four plates. Divide the chicken tenders among the plates and serve hot.

FANCY LAMB CHOPS
WITH CRISPY POTATOES AND MINT SALAD

3 tablespoons **olive oil**

1 tablespoon **unsalted butter**

8 **lamb rib chops** (1¾ pounds total)

Kosher salt and **freshly ground black pepper**

1½ pounds **new potatoes**, cut into ¼-inch-thick coins

4 **garlic cloves**, peeled and smashed

¼ **shallot**, thinly sliced

1 tablespoon **red wine vinegar**

½ cup lightly packed **fresh mint** leaves, coarsely chopped

½ cup lightly packed **fresh flat-leaf parsley**, coarsely chopped

¼ cup thinly sliced **fresh chives**

Think "fancy" and "fewer than 20 minutes" don't go together? Think again, fancypants! Lamb and mint are a classic combination, so much so that this calls for an obligatory dad joke: How is mint like an escaped bank robber? They're both on the lam! But seriously: This simple mint salad is the perfect complement to the rich lamb chops and crispy potatoes. Go ahead—make your weeknight dinner a little extra.

1 Heat 2 tablespoons olive oil and the butter in a large skillet over medium-high heat. Season the lamb chops all over with salt and pepper, then add them to the skillet and cook until browned on the outside and cooked medium inside, about 6 minutes, flipping once halfway through. Transfer the chops to a plate and tent with foil to keep warm.

2 Return the skillet to high heat and add the potatoes and garlic. Stir to coat them with the fat in the skillet, season with salt and pepper, and cook, stirring occasionally, until tender and lightly browned, 12 to 14 minutes.

3 While the potatoes are cooking, combine the shallot and vinegar in a medium bowl and let sit for 5 minutes. Add the remaining 1 tablespoon olive oil, the mint, parsley, and chives and season with salt and pepper. Toss the salad together to coat the herbs with the dressing.

4 Remove the skillet from the heat and divide the potatoes among four plates. Place 2 chops on each plate, top with some of the mint salad, and serve.

BAKED POTATO *and* PEA
DINNER SAMOSAS

SERVES 4

Traditional samosas are deep-fried, but we're lightening things up with this oven-baked version. Each one is a little pouch of peas, potatoes, and traditional Indian flavors (meaning the flavors will develop more fully over time—perfect for meal prep!). Supplement them with extra veggies or protein, and you'll transform this classic Indian snack into meals for days.

<‹••••••••••••••••›>

3 tablespoons **vegetable oil**, plus more for brushing

1 teaspoon **brown mustard seeds**

1 medium **yellow onion**, finely chopped

1 **serrano chile**, seeded and minced (optional)

1 teaspoon **garam masala**

1 teaspoon **ground coriander**

½ teaspoon **ground cumin**

½ teaspoon **ground turmeric**

½ teaspoon **sweet paprika**

3 **garlic cloves**, minced

1 pound **russet potatoes**, peeled, boiled, and cut into ½-inch chunks

1 cup **frozen peas**, thawed

2 tablespoons **fresh lemon juice**

Kosher salt and **freshly ground black pepper**

All-purpose flour, for dusting

1 pound **store-bought pizza dough**

Mango, coriander, and/or **tamarind chutneys**, for serving

1 Heat the vegetable oil in a medium saucepan over medium-high heat. Add the mustard seeds and cook until they begin popping, about 1 minute. Add the onion and chile (if using) and cook, stirring, until caramelized, 8 to 10 minutes. Stir in the garam masala, coriander, cumin, turmeric, paprika, and garlic and cook, stirring, until fragrant, about 1 minute more.

2 Add the potatoes, peas, and lemon juice and stir until the potatoes are evenly coated with the spice mixture and onions. Remove the pan from the heat and season with salt and pepper. Let the mixture cool.

3 Preheat the oven to 425°F.

4 On a lightly floured work surface, divide the pizza dough into 4 equal portions. Roll and stretch each portion into a 7-inch round. Place one-quarter of the cooled filling in the center of each round. Using a pastry brush, brush the edge of one-half of each dough round with water, then fold the dry dough half over to create half-moons. Press the edges together all the way around, then crimp with a fork to seal securely.

5 Brush the tops of the samosas lightly with more oil, then bake until golden brown on the outside and the filling is warmed through, 20 to 25 minutes. Serve hot, with chutney on the side.

EAT IT FOUR DIFFERENT WAYS

MAKE IT

MEAL PREP

day ①

Serve with sautéed shrimp on the side.

day ②

Serve with spinach sautéed with garlic and red pepper flakes.

Cut open and place quarters of soft-cooked egg into each samosa.

Place 2 slices of Swiss cheese over each samosa and reheat in the oven to melt the cheese on top.

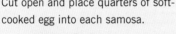

day ③

day ④

SWEET-AND-SOUR PORK

SERVES 4

2 pounds boneless **pork shoulder**, cut into ¾-inch chunks

½ cup **soy sauce**

¼ cup thinly sliced **scallions**, plus more for garnish

1 teaspoon **freshly ground black pepper**

2 **garlic cloves**, minced

2 tablespoons **vegetable oil**, plus more for frying

3 large **eggs**, beaten

1½ cups **cornstarch**

1 small **white onion**, cut into ¾-inch chunks

1 **red bell pepper**, stemmed and cut into ¾-inch chunks

1 **green bell pepper**, stemmed and cut into ¾-inch chunks

1 cup chopped canned **pineapple**, drained

¼ cup **rice vinegar**

¼ cup **sugar**

¼ cup **ketchup**

Cooked white rice, for serving

Crispy, sweet, and savory, this Chinese takeout classic is so satisfying, you might be tempted to swear off takeout for good. When you're deep-frying your pork, make sure to keep an eye on the deep-fry thermometer—in order to keep the temperature at 350°F, you may need to take a short break between batches (if the temperature isn't high enough, the pork will take longer to cook and may get soggy). Don't stress, though—once you get started, you're going to be itching to fry, fry again.

1   Combine the pork, ¼ cup of the soy sauce, the scallions, pepper, and garlic in a large bowl. Cover with plastic wrap and marinate in the refrigerator for at least 30 minutes or preferably up to 2 hours.

2   Fill a large saucepan with vegetable oil to a depth of 2 inches. Attach a deep-fry thermometer to the side of the pan and heat the oil over medium-high heat to 350°F.

3   Pour the eggs into a medium bowl and place the cornstarch in a separate medium bowl. Working in batches of 10 to 12 pieces, dip the pork in the egg, then toss in the cornstarch to coat. Add the coated pork to the hot oil and fry, stirring, until crisp and golden brown, 3 to 4 minutes. Using a slotted spoon or spider, transfer the pork to paper towels to drain.

4   In a wok or large skillet, heat the 2 tablespoons vegetable oil over medium-high heat. Add the onion and bell peppers and cook, stirring, until crisp-tender, 6 to 8 minutes. Stir in the pineapple, then add the remaining ¼ cup soy sauce, the vinegar, sugar, and ketchup and cook, stirring continuously, until the sauce thickens, about 5 minutes.

5   Return the pork to the pan and toss to coat evenly with the sauce. Remove the pan from the heat and sprinkle the pork with more scallions. Serve the pork hot, with rice.

JUICY LUCY BURGERS

2 pounds **ground beef**

2 teaspoons **onion powder**

2 teaspoons **kosher salt**

1 teaspoon **freshly ground black pepper**

4 ounces **Cheddar cheese**, cut into 6 chunks

2 tablespoons **vegetable oil**

6 **hamburger buns**

6 slices **bacon**, cooked and cut in half crosswise

6 slices **tomato**

6 **lettuce leaves**

The Juicy Lucy burger was created in Minnesota, but news of its deliciousness has spread far and wide. It's essentially an inside-out cheeseburger. By wrapping chunks of Cheddar in your ground beef before cooking it, you create an ooey-gooey liquid center. Add some smoky bacon, and you've got a surefire crowd-pleaser on your hands (or preferably *in* your hands).

1 Combine the ground beef, onion powder, salt, and pepper in a large bowl and mix with your hands until the seasonings are fully incorporated and mixed throughout the meat. Divide the seasoned beef into 6 equal portions and form each into a flat patty.

2 Place a chunk of Cheddar in the center of each patty and wrap the beef around it completely. Re-form the beef into a patty with your hands.

3 Heat 1 tablespoon of the vegetable oil in a medium cast-iron skillet over medium-high heat. Add 3 patties and cook until browned on both sides and cooked through in the center, 8 to 10 minutes, flipping once halfway through. Transfer the patties to a plate and repeat with the remaining 1 tablespoon oil to cook the remaining 3 patties.

4 While the burgers are hot, place each on a bun and top with 2 pieces of the bacon, a slice of tomato, and a lettuce leaf. Serve immediately.

EGG ROLLS

SERVES 4

3½ ounces **glass or cellophane (bean thread) noodles**

2 cups shredded **green cabbage**

½ cup finely chopped **scallions**

3 tablespoons **soy sauce**

1 tablespoon **toasted sesame oil**

1 teaspoon **onion powder**

1 teaspoon **garlic powder**

1 teaspoon **freshly ground black pepper**

½ teaspoon **kosher salt**

1 large **carrot**, shredded

8 ounces extra-large (16/20-count) **shrimp**, peeled, deveined, and coarsely chopped

8 ounces **ground pork**

16 wheat **egg roll wrappers**

Vegetable oil, for frying

Cooked white rice, for serving

Asian sweet chili sauce, for dipping

You might be used to seeing egg rolls as an appetizer, but we think they deserve center stage. These shrimp-and-pork rolls combine all the elements of a complete dinner: protein, veggies, carbs, and—of course—plenty of flavor. Luckily, this recipe serves four, so you can keep the "Leggo my egg rolls!" to a minimum.

1 Place the noodles in a large bowl and add enough boiling water to cover them. Let sit for 10 minutes to soften. Drain the noodles, chop them into ½-inch pieces A , and return them to the bowl. Stir in the cabbage, scallions, soy sauce, sesame oil, onion powder, garlic powder, pepper, salt, and carrot. Add the shrimp and pork B and mix until evenly combined.

2 Place an egg roll wrapper on a clean work surface and scoop a level ¼ cup of the filling into the center C . Fold the bottom of the wrapper over the filling, then fold in the sides D and roll tightly to enclose the filling. Using your finger, lightly wet the inner tip of the wrapper and continue rolling to seal the egg roll. Repeat with the remaining wrappers and filling.

3 Fill a large saucepan with vegetable oil to a depth of 2 inches. Attach a deep-fry thermometer to the side of the pan and heat the oil over medium-high heat to 350°F. Working in batches of four, carefully add the egg rolls to the hot oil and fry until crispy and golden brown, 5 to 6 minutes. Using a slotted spoon, transfer the egg rolls to a wire rack or plate lined with paper towels to drain E . Repeat to cook the remaining egg rolls.

4 Serve the egg rolls hot, with rice alongside and sweet chili sauce for dipping.

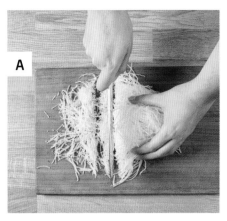

MARGHERITA FRENCH BREAD PIZZAS

1 large loaf **French bread** (at least 20 inches long)

2 cups homemade or store-bought **tomato sauce**

1½ cups shredded **low-moisture mozzarella cheese**

8 ounces **mini fresh mozzarella balls**, halved

12 **cherry tomatoes**, halved

Kosher salt and **freshly ground black pepper**

2 tablespoons finely chopped **fresh basil leaves**

Crushed red pepper flakes, for serving

Our favorite kind of life hack is a pizza-based life hack, so we decided to be the change we wished to see at the dinner table! These French bread pizzas combine the ease of a sandwich with the cheesy magic of a Margherita pizza. Bypass the crusty baguette for this one in favor of a larger—and softer—French loaf.

1 Preheat the oven to 350°F. Line a baking sheet with parchment paper.

2 Using a serrated knife, slice the bread in half crosswise, then slice each half lengthwise through its equator to make 4 pieces total. Arrange the bread pieces on the prepared baking sheet, cut-side up.

3 Divide the tomato sauce evenly among the bread pieces, then sprinkle them with the shredded mozzarella, dividing it evenly. Top with the fresh mozzarella and cherry tomato halves, then season with salt and black pepper.

4 Bake until the cheese is melted and bubbling and the bread is crisp at the edges, 10 to 12 minutes. Remove the pizzas from the oven, sprinkle with basil and red pepper flakes, and serve.

TACO-NIGHT CRUNCH WRAP

3 tablespoons **olive oil**

3 medium **white onions**, finely chopped

Kosher salt and **freshly ground black pepper**

3 pounds 90% lean **ground beef**

¼ cup finely chopped **fresh cilantro**

3 vine-ripe **tomatoes**, finely chopped

3 (1-ounce) packets **taco seasoning**

¼ cup fresh **lime juice**

Nonstick cooking spray

8 burrito-size **flour tortillas**, warmed

3 cups shredded **Cheddar cheese**

3 cups shredded **Monterey Jack cheese**

5 **corn tostadas**

Sour cream and **salsa**, for serving

This fast food favorite might look simple, but it's got *layers*. Layers of flavorful beef, double cheese, and crunchy tostadas, to be precise. It's perfect for parties, game days, or just your average mega-hungry week night. Go ahead and go for seconds or thirds: this is a judgment-free zone.

1 Heat the olive oil in a large Dutch oven over medium-high heat. Add the onions, season with salt and pepper, and cook, stirring occasionally, until caramelized, 10 to 12 minutes. Add the ground beef and cook, stirring to break it up as it cooks, until no longer pink, 8 to 10 minutes. Add the cilantro, tomatoes, taco seasoning, and lime juice and stir until evenly combined. Remove the skillet from the heat and let cool.

2 Preheat the oven to 375°F. Generously spray a large (13 by 18-inch) rimmed baking sheet with cooking spray.

3 Orient the prepared baking sheet so its long sides run parallel in front of you. Place 1 tortilla in the center on the left-hand side of the baking sheet so it is half on the sheet and half on the counter. Working clockwise, place 2 more tortillas along the top side of the baking sheet so they overlap evenly to cover the whole top edge A . Place 1 tortilla in the center of the right-hand side of the baking sheet, then place 2 more tortillas along the bottom edge of the baking sheet so they meet with the first tortilla. Place 1 tortilla in the center of the baking sheet to cover the gap B .

4 Sprinkle half of each cheese evenly over the portions of the tortillas that are covering just the bottom of the baking sheet. Use a slotted spoon to scoop the beef mixture onto the cheese and spread it into an even layer. Arrange the tostadas evenly over the beef, with one in each of the four corners and one placed in the center C . Sprinkle the remaining cheeses evenly over the tostadas. Starting with the first tortilla on your left-hand side, fold the overhanging tortilla edges back over

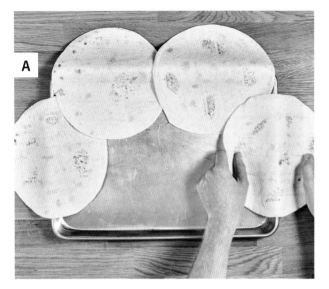

the filling so they cover the filling D . Place the remaining tortilla over the cheese in the center of the baking sheet. Spray the tortillas with cooking spray.

5. Place another baking sheet on top of the crunch wrap, then place an ovenproof weight like a large cast-iron skillet on top of the baking sheet. Bake for 30 minutes, then remove the weight and top baking sheet and bake until the tortillas are golden and crisp on top, about 15 minutes more.

Remove the baking sheet from the oven and set it on a wire rack. Let rest for 5 minutes.

6. Using oven mitts or kitchen towels to protect your hands, place a cutting board upside down over the crunch wrap, then, holding the cutting board and baking sheet together, flip them so the crunch wrap falls out of the baking sheet onto the cutting board. Remove the baking sheet and cut the crunch wrap into 8 squares. Serve with sour cream and salsa on the side.

ARROZ CON POLLO

SERVES 4

2 tablespoons **vegetable oil**

4 bone-in, skin-on **chicken legs** (thigh and drumstick attached)

Kosher salt and **freshly ground black pepper**

1 large **white onion**, minced

1 small **red bell pepper**, stemmed, seeded, and minced

3 **garlic cloves**, minced

¼ teaspoon **crushed red pepper flakes**

1 **bay leaf**

1 (15-ounce) can diced **tomatoes**

1 (15-ounce) can **red kidney beans**, drained and rinsed

1 cup **long-grain white rice**, rinsed

1 cup low-sodium **chicken stock**

Fresh cilantro leaves, for garnish (optional)

Arroz con pollo is (with respect to our dear friends rice and chicken) so much greater than the sum of its parts. A traditional dish in Spain and Latin America, *arroz con pollo* is a deceptively simple, incredibly flavorful dish. Our version includes kidney beans to make it a little more substantial. Warm, filling, and one-pot? Everything's comin' up ar-*roses*!

1 Preheat the oven to 425°F.

2 Heat the vegetable oil in a large high-sided skillet over medium-high heat. Season the chicken with salt and pepper, then add 2 chicken legs to the skillet, skin-side down, and cook, undisturbed, until the skin is golden brown and the fat has rendered, about 8 minutes. Using tongs, transfer the chicken pieces to a plate, skin-side up. Repeat with the remaining 2 chicken legs.

3 Return the skillet to medium-high heat. Add the onion, bell pepper, garlic, red pepper flakes, and bay leaf and cook, stirring, until the vegetables are softened, 6 to 8 minutes. Stir in the tomatoes and their juices, beans, and rice and season with salt and pepper.

4 Pour in the stock and stir to combine. Return the chicken legs to the skillet, skin-side up, and bring the sauce to a simmer. Reduce the heat to medium-low to maintain a gentle simmer, cover the skillet, and cook until the rice and chicken are both cooked through and tender, 20 to 25 minutes.

5 Remove the skillet from the heat and let sit, covered, for 5 minutes. Uncover and discard the bay leaf. Garnish with cilantro, if you like, before serving.

GENERAL TSO'S CHICKEN

SERVES 4

SAUCE

1⅓ cups **chicken stock**

⅓ cup **rice vinegar**

⅓ cup **tomato paste**

¼ cup **soy sauce**

¼ cup **sugar**

1 tablespoon **cornstarch**

CHICKEN

2½ pounds boneless, skinless **chicken thighs**, cut into 1-inch cubes

6 tablespoons **cornstarch**

2 tablespoons **vegetable oil**, plus more for deep-frying

2 tablespoons **soy sauce**

3 large **egg yolks**

6 **garlic cloves**, minced

1 (1-inch) piece **fresh ginger**, peeled and minced

8 dried **chiles de árbol**

2 teaspoons **toasted sesame oil**

Thinly sliced **scallions**, for garnish
Cooked white rice, for serving

General Tso's chicken is as much a staple of Chinese takeout as fortune cookies. Lightly battered, sweet, and spicy, it's compulsively munchable. And if we do say so ourselves, our version is one of the best we've ever tasted. Our secret? Plenty of rice vinegar in the sauce, to keep the flavors balanced and prevent the sweetness from overpowering your palate. The only problem? Your favorite Chinese restaurant might start to feel a little neglected.

1 Make the sauce: Whisk together the stock, vinegar, tomato paste, soy sauce, sugar, and cornstarch in a medium bowl until smooth. Set aside.

2 Make the chicken: Place the chicken, cornstarch, 2 tablespoons of the vegetable oil, the soy sauce, and the egg yolks in a large resealable plastic bag. Seal the bag and massage the chicken until it's completely coated in the batter. Set aside.

3 Fill a large high-sided skillet with vegetable oil to a depth of 2 inches. Attach a deep-fry thermometer to the side of the pan and heat the oil over medium-high heat to 375°F. Working in batches, add the chicken to the hot oil and fry, tossing, until golden brown and cooked through, about 5 minutes. Using a spider or slotted spoon, transfer the chicken to paper towels to drain. Remove the pan from the heat and carefully pour off all but 3 tablespoons of the oil from the pan; remove the thermometer, too.

4 Return the pan to medium-high heat. Add the garlic, ginger, and chile and cook, stirring, until starting to brown, about 1 minute. Pour in the sauce and sesame oil and cook, stirring, until the mixture has reduced slightly and thickened to a thin gravy, 8 to 10 minutes. Return the chicken to the pot and cook, tossing it in the sauce, to warm through, 1 to 2 minutes.

5 Transfer the chicken and sauce to a platter and sprinkle with the scallions. Serve hot, with rice.

JAMAICAN BEEF "PATTY PIE"

1½ pounds **ground beef**

Kosher salt

4 **garlic cloves**, minced

2 small **yellow onions**, finely chopped

1 **habanero or Scotch bonnet chile**, seeded (if desired) and finely chopped

¼ cup **curry powder**

3 tablespoons **fresh thyme leaves**, chopped

1½ teaspoons **ground allspice**

Freshly ground black pepper

3 tablespoons **all-purpose flour**, plus more for dusting

2 cups **beef stock**

1 sheet store-bought **puff pastry**, thawed if frozen

2 tablespoons **whole milk**

¼ teaspoon **ground turmeric** (optional)

1 large **egg**

Fresh cilantro leaves and **plain yogurt** (optional), for serving

The Jamaican beef patty is a popular on-the-go meal in Jamaica (and New York City, luckily for us on the Tasty team!). We've borrowed its delicious flavors to create a potpie-style version. Scotch bonnet peppers are a popular ingredient in Jamaican cuisine, but feel free to swap in a habanero if you can't find them. Oh, and a word about frozen puff pastry: Thawing it in the fridge the night before will make it much easier to work with.

1 Heat a large saucepan over medium-high heat. Add the beef, season with salt, and cook, stirring, until no longer pink, 6 to 8 minutes. Add the garlic, onions, and chile and cook, stirring, until the vegetables are soft, the beef is browned, and no liquid remains in the pan, 8 to 10 minutes.

2 Stir in the curry powder, thyme, and allspice; season with salt and pepper; and cook, stirring, until toasted and fragrant, about 2 minutes. Add the flour and cook, stirring, for 1 minute. Stir in the stock, bring it to a simmer, and cook, stirring, until thickened, 2 to 3 minutes. Remove from the heat and let cool.

3 Preheat the oven to 425°F. Line a baking sheet with foil.

4 On a work surface, roll the puff pastry into an 11-inch square, then trim it into an 11-inch round. Pour the beef filling into a 9½- to 10-inch deep-dish pie pan or baking dish. Top with the puff pastry circle and carefully press it along the edges of the pan to seal. Using a paring knife, cut a few slits in the top of the pastry to release steam.

5 Whisk together the milk, turmeric (if using), and egg in a small bowl. Using a pastry brush, brush the pastry with some of the egg wash. Place the pie on the prepared baking sheet and bake until golden brown on top and bubbling in the center, 25 to 30 minutes.

6 Remove the pie from the oven and let cool for 10 minutes. Sprinkle with cilantro, if desired, and serve with yogurt.

MUSHROOM-AND-BEAN VEGGIE BURGERS

BURGER PATTIES

4 tablespoons **vegetable oil**

8 ounces **button mushrooms**, finely chopped

1 **garlic clove**, minced

Kosher salt and **freshly ground black pepper**

1 tablespoon **soy sauce**

½ teaspoon **smoked paprika**

1 (15-ounce) can **black beans**, drained and rinsed

½ cup **plain bread crumbs**

¼ cup finely chopped **fresh flat-leaf parsley**

1 tablespoon **fresh lemon juice**

FIXIN'S

6 slices regular or vegan **American cheese**

6 **hamburger buns**

Mayonnaise, **mustard**, and/or **ketchup**, for serving

Shredded **iceberg lettuce**, diced **white onion**, **dill pickle chips**, and sliced **tomato**, for serving

With the right combination of ingredients, making your own veggie burgers can be even easier than hitting the drive-through (and the finished product is definitely easier on your body)! Mushrooms give the patties a meaty texture; soy sauce, garlic, and paprika add a zesty flavor; and black beans and bread crumbs bind everything together. Add some classic burger fixin's and we're pretty sure you won't even miss the meat (though you might still want fries with that—hey, you're only human).

1   Heat 2 tablespoons of the vegetable oil in a large skillet over medium heat. Add the mushrooms and garlic, season with salt and pepper, and cook, stirring occasionally, until the mushrooms are golden brown and all the liquid they release has evaporated, about 10 minutes. Stir in the soy sauce and paprika and cook for 30 seconds more. Remove the pan from the heat.

2   Place the beans in a medium bowl and mash them lightly with a potato masher or fork. Stir in the mushroom mixture, bread crumbs, parsley, and lemon juice. Season with salt and pepper, and mix until evenly combined.

3   Line a baking sheet with parchment paper. Using your hands, divide the mixture into 6 portions and shape each into a 3½-inch-round, ½-inch-thick patty. Place the patties on the prepared baking sheet and refrigerate for at least 20 minutes.

4   Heat the remaining 2 tablespoons oil in a large skillet over medium heat. Add the patties and cook until golden brown and warmed through, 8 to 10 minutes, flipping once halfway through. If using cheese, top each patty with a cheese slice after you flip it.

5   While the burgers are warm, place one on each bun and top with condiments and veggie fixin's. Serve immediately.

COOK

SOUTHWESTERN SALAD
with AVOCADO DRESSING

If you're on the hunt for a substantial, protein-rich salad, look no further than this Southwestern-style salad. Your blender is your passport to salad dressing paradise, and once you try our creamy avocado-cilantro version, you might just swear off store-bought varieties for good. To maximize your salad's meal-prep potential, store the dressing separately in a small jar or covered plastic container so your greens don't wilt.

<‹••••••••••••••›>

DRESSING

¼ cup **olive oil**

1 tablespoon **fresh cilantro leaves**

½ teaspoon **kosher salt**

½ teaspoon **freshly ground black pepper**

1 **avocado**, halved, pitted, and peeled

Juice of 1 lime

1 **garlic clove**

SALAD

1 head **romaine lettuce**, chopped

1 cup chopped **bell peppers**

¾ cup chopped **tomato**

½ cup chopped **red onion**

¼ cup thinly sliced **scallions**

¼ cup **fresh cilantro leaves**

1 (15-ounce) can **black beans**, drained and rinsed

1 (15-ounce) can **corn**, drained and rinsed

1 Make the dressing: In a blender, combine the olive oil, cilantro, salt, pepper, avocado, lime juice, and garlic and blend until smooth.

2 Make the salad: Place the lettuce in the bottom of a large bowl. Keeping each ingredient separate from the others, arrange piles of the bell peppers, tomato, red onion, scallions, cilantro, beans, and corn over the lettuce.

3 Drizzle the dressing over the salad and toss to coat before serving.

EAT IT FOUR DIFFERENT WAYS

MAKE IT

MEAL PREP

day ①

Serve the salad with a fillet of cold poached salmon or chicken.

day ②

Sprinkle ½ cup crumbled tortilla chips over the top just before serving.

Spoon the salad onto a warmed large flour tortilla and wrap it up to make a salad burrito.

Stir in ½ cup cooked quinoa before adding the dressing.

day ④

day ③

WATERMELON SALAD
WITH SPINACH AND MANGO

SERVES
4 TO 6

1 small (4½-pound) **watermelon**

2 tablespoons **extra-virgin olive oil**

2 tablespoons **fresh lemon juice**

1 tablespoon **honey**

Kosher salt and **freshly ground black pepper**

3 cups **baby spinach** (3 ounces)

½ cup slivered **almonds**

1 large **mango**, pitted, peeled, and cut into ½-inch cubes

We're calling it: this thoroughly refreshing salad is the perfect meal for those hot summer days when just the idea of turning on a stove makes you start sweating. A dressing of olive oil, lemon juice, and honey—so deliciously simple, we could call it an *un*dressing—is all you need for this light-and-bright combination of spinach and summer fruits, while slivered almonds add the perfect amount of texture.

1 Using a sharp knife, cut off the top and bottom of the watermelon to reveal the red flesh and create flat surfaces on both sides. Stand the watermelon upright and slice off the remaining rind so only the pink core remains. Cut the watermelon into roughly 1-inch cubes and transfer to a large bowl.

2 Whisk together the olive oil, lemon juice, honey, and 1 tablespoon water in a small bowl and season with salt and pepper.

3 Add the spinach, almonds, and mango to the bowl with the watermelon. Pour the dressing on top and gently toss to combine.

4 Divide the salad among bowls and serve.

AVOCADO TOAST 4 WAYS

MAKES 4 TOASTS EACH

Avocado toast has been the butt of a lot of jokes in the past few years—yes, we've all heard the one about millennials not being able to buy houses because they've spent all their money on it—so we thought it needed a little bit of an image overhaul. We created four spins on the classic—peach and feta, hummus and cucumber, caprese, and BLT—that showcase the versatility of the humble avocado. Because avocados—like millennials—should never be underestimated!

CAPRESE

4 slices **bread**
2 **avocados**, pitted, peeled, and mashed
Kosher salt and **freshly ground black pepper**
4 vine-ripe or heirloom **tomatoes**, thinly sliced
1 large ball **fresh mozzarella cheese**,
cut into 8 slices
¼ cup lightly packed **fresh basil leaves**,
thinly sliced

1 Toast the bread slices in a toaster or toaster oven.

2 Divide the mashed avocado evenly among the
   toast slices, spread it evenly over the top of each,
   and season with salt and pepper. Divide the
   tomato slices evenly among the toasts and top
   each with 2 slices of the mozzarella.

3 Sprinkle each toast with one-quarter of the basil
   and serve.

PEACH AND FETA

4 slices **bread**
2 **avocados**, pitted, peeled, and thinly sliced
2 ripe **peaches**, pitted and thinly sliced
4 tablespoons crumbled **feta cheese**

1 Toast the bread slices in a toaster or toaster oven.

2 Alternately arrange slices from ½ avocado and
   ½ peach over each piece of toast.

3 Sprinkle each toast with 1 tablespoon of the feta
   and serve.

BLT

4 slices **bread**
2 **avocados**, pitted, peeled, and mashed
Kosher salt and **freshly ground black pepper**
2 vine-ripe or heirloom **tomatoes**, thickly sliced
½ cup shredded **romaine or green-leaf lettuce**
4 slices **bacon**, cooked and coarsely crumbled

1 Toast the bread slices in a toaster or toaster oven.

2 Divide the mashed avocado evenly among the
   toast slices, spread it evenly over the top of each,
   and season with salt and pepper. Divide the
   tomato slices evenly among the toasts and top
   each with one-quarter of the lettuce.

3 Sprinkle each toast with one-quarter of the
   bacon and serve.

HUMMUS AND CUCUMBER

4 slices **bread**
½ cup **hummus**
24 thin slices **cucumber**
2 **avocados**, pitted, peeled, and thinly sliced
Kosher salt and **freshly ground black pepper**

1 Toast the bread slices in a toaster or toaster oven.

2 Spread 2 tablespoons of the hummus on each
   slice of toast, then top each piece with 6 slices of
   the cucumber and ½ sliced avocado.

3 Season the toasts with salt and pepper and serve.

CURRIED ROTISSERIE CHICKEN
WALDORF SALAD

1 rotisserie **chicken**

1 cup **mayonnaise**

1 cup **sour cream**

1 cup **mango chutney**, preferably Major Grey's

1½ tablespoons **curry powder**

1 cup halved **green grapes**

¾ cup diced (½-inch) **tart apple**

½ cup coarsely chopped **walnuts**

2 **celery stalks**, halved lengthwise, then thinly sliced crosswise

Kosher salt and **freshly ground black pepper**

Lettuce or **bread slices**, for serving

Invented at the Waldorf Hotel in the late 1800s, this salad has stood the test of time—but even classics can benefit from a little upgrade now and then! We've added curry powder and mango chutney to our version to give it an extra pop of flavor. Eat it with lettuce for a traditional Waldorf salad experience, or give it the sandwich treatment—either way, this salad is a class act.

1 Pick the meat from the rotisserie chicken and cut it into ½-inch chunks; discard the skin and bones.

2 Whisk together the mayonnaise, sour cream, chutney, and curry powder in a large bowl until smooth. Add the chopped chicken, grapes, apple, walnuts, and celery and toss to combine. Season the chicken salad with salt and pepper.

3 Serve the chicken salad on top of lettuce for a salad or between two slices of bread for a sandwich.

MARINATED CHOPPED SALAD

SERVES 6

1 **garlic clove**

Kosher salt

½ cup **extra-virgin olive oil**

¼ cup **red wine vinegar**

2 teaspoons chopped **fresh thyme leaves**

½ teaspoon **dried oregano**

¼ teaspoon **crushed red pepper flakes**

4 ounces **mozzarella cheese**, drained and cut into ½-inch chunks

4 ounces deli-sliced **provolone cheese**, cut into ¼-inch-wide strips

4 ounces **deli-sliced salami**, cut into ¼-inch-wide strips

2 bunches **kale**, stems and ribs removed, leaves coarsely chopped (about 2 cups)

1 (15-ounce) can **chickpeas**, drained and rinsed

1 **shallot**, thinly sliced

Freshly ground black pepper

1 head **radicchio**, cored and coarsely chopped

1 **avocado**, halved, pitted, peeled, and cut into ¼-inch chunks

Grated **Parmesan cheese**, for serving (optional)

This salad is basically a deli counter in a bowl, and we can't get enough of it. Classic Italian herbs, cheese, and charcuterie anchor the flavors in the classic chopped salad tradition, while kale, radicchio, and avocado add a little bit of California freshness to the mix. This salad is so big and hearty, the only thing you'll wish for is a bigger bowl.

1 Mince the garlic on a cutting board, then sprinkle with a pinch of salt and chop and scrape the garlic and the salt back and forth with the flat side of the knife until it forms a mostly smooth paste. (This technique makes it easier for the garlic to disperse in the dressing and also tames the harsh flavor of the raw garlic.)

2 Scrape the garlic paste into a large bowl and whisk in the olive oil, vinegar, thyme, oregano, and red pepper flakes. Add the mozzarella, provolone, salami, kale, chickpeas, and shallot and season with salt and pepper. Toss to combine, then gently stir in the radicchio and avocado.

3 Divide the salad among six bowls, sprinkle with Parmesan, if you like, and serve.

GREEK CAPRESE SALAD

2 large heirloom or vine-ripe **tomatoes**, cored and cut into ¼-inch-thick slices

1¼ pounds **fresh mozzarella cheese**, cut into ¼-inch-thick slices

¼ **English cucumber**, halved lengthwise, seeded, and cut into ¼-inch cubes

⅓ cup pitted **kalamata olives**, halved

¼ cup **extra-virgin olive oil**

2 tablespoons **red wine vinegar**

½ teaspoon **dried oregano**

½ teaspoon **dried basil**

Kosher salt and **freshly ground black pepper**

½ **shallot**, thinly sliced lengthwise

2 ounces **feta cheese**, finely crumbled

This salad brings together elements of two of our favorite salads: caprese (a simple combination of tomato, mozzarella, and basil, usually served with balsamic vinegar and olive oil) and Greek. Tomatoes are the star of the show here—though two kinds of cheese are worthy supporting characters—so this is a particularly great choice for dinner in high summer, which is peak tomato season. With the best elements from a Greek favorite and an Italian one, this salad is a true Mediterranean power pairing.

1 Arrange the tomatoes and mozzarella on a platter in an alternating fashion, overlapping them slightly to cover the bottom. Top with the cucumber and olives.

2 Whisk together the olive oil, vinegar, oregano, and basil in a small bowl. Season the dressing with salt and pepper, then add the shallot and toss to coat. Let the shallot stand in the dressing for 5 minutes.

3 Using a fork, retrieve the shallots from the dressing and sprinkle them over the salad. Drizzle the dressing evenly over the salad, then sprinkle with the feta and serve.

VEGAN THREE-BEAN-AND-HERB POWER SALAD

WITH CREAMY RANCH

RANCH DRESSING

1 cup raw **cashews**

Boiling water

⅔ cup **unsweetened almond milk**

2 teaspoons **fresh lemon juice**

2 tablespoons **apple cider vinegar**

½ small **shallot**

1 **garlic clove**

2 tablespoons minced **fresh dill**

2 tablespoons minced **fresh flat-leaf parsley**

2 teaspoons minced **fresh chives**

Kosher salt and **freshly ground black pepper**

BEAN SALAD

1 (15-ounce) can **cannellini beans**, drained and rinsed

1 (15-ounce) can **chickpeas**, drained and rinsed

1 (15-ounce) can **pink beans**, drained and rinsed

1 **English cucumber**, halved lengthwise, seeded, and thinly sliced crosswise

¼ cup coarsely chopped **fresh dill**, plus more to garnish

¼ cup coarsely chopped **fresh flat-leaf parsley**

¼ cup chopped (½-inch lengths) **fresh chives**

Lettuce leaves or **toast**, for serving

This salad's strength derives from the power of three—three beans, that is. We love a legume, so three of them together is basically a bean dream come true. And while ranch dressing usually relies on buttermilk and mayo for its characteristic creaminess, our vegan version uses almond milk and cashews to achieve a similar texture. Soaking your cashews before use softens them, making them milder and easier to blend. Make a little extra dressing and use it throughout the week as a veggie dip!

1   Make the ranch dressing: Place the cashews in a small bowl and add boiling water to cover. Let the cashews soak for 30 minutes. Meanwhile, combine the almond milk and lemon juice in a blender and let stand to curdle, making vegan "buttermilk."

2   Drain and rinse the cashews, then transfer them to the blender with the almond milk mixture. Add the vinegar, shallot, and garlic. Puree the mixture until very smooth. Pour the dressing into a bowl and stir in the dill, parsley, and chives. Season with salt and pepper. Cover and refrigerate until ready to use. (The dressing will keep for up to 5 days.)

3   Make the bean salad: Combine the cannellini beans, chickpeas, pink beans, cucumber, dill, parsley, and chives in a large bowl. Add the ranch dressing and toss to coat the salad. Divide the salad among four bowls and sprinkle each with more dill. Serve on lettuce or with toast.

RAINBOW VEGGIE SALAD

WITH HONEY-MUSTARD DRESSING

1 large head **romaine or green-leaf lettuce**, coarsely chopped

2 cups **cherry tomatoes** or **grape tomatoes**, halved

2 cups shredded **carrots**

2 yellow **bell peppers**, finely chopped

1 **English cucumber**, halved, seeded, and thinly sliced

1 medium **red onion**, finely chopped

3 tablespoons **olive oil**

3 tablespoons **red wine vinegar**

3 tablespoons **honey**

3 tablespoons **Dijon mustard**

1 tablespoon **dried oregano**

1 **garlic clove**, minced

Kosher salt and **freshly ground black pepper**

We've heard that you eat with your eyes first, and there's something so appetizing about this gloriously multihued salad. With lettuce, tomatoes, carrots, bell peppers, cucumber, and onion, it's a veritable garden in a bowl (a garden with honey-mustard dressing—our favorite kind!). When you're preparing your cucumber, halve it lengthwise and run the side of a spoon down the center of the cut side to remove the seeds.

1 Combine the lettuce, tomatoes, carrots, bell peppers, cucumber, and onion in a large bowl.

2 Whisk together the olive oil, vinegar, honey, mustard, oregano, and garlic in a medium bowl and season with salt and pepper.

3 Just before serving, pour the dressing over the salad and toss to combine.

BOWLS

AROUND-THE-WORLD FRIED RICE

Fried rice is a gift from the gods of meal prep. Seriously: It's quick, it's one-pot, it actually tastes better made with cold, day-old rice (as fresh-cooked rice has a tendency to get a bit soggy), and there are pretty much infinite variations. Here are just four examples—each one representing a different type of cuisine—but feel free to experiment with different proteins and vegetables! Think of leftover rice as the blank canvas on which to create your masterpiece. Your delicious, delicious masterpiece.

‹ • • • • • • • • • • • • • • ›

EAT IT FOUR DIFFERENT WAYS

CHINESE-STYLE

Heat 2 tablespoons vegetable oil in a large skillet over high heat. Add 1 cup cooled cooked long-grain white rice, ½ cup frozen peas, and 2 minced scallions and cook, stirring, until the rice is browned and crisp, 3 to 4 minutes. Move the rice to one side of the skillet, crack 1 large egg into the empty space, then cook, stirring everything together again, until the egg is cooked, 2 minutes. Transfer to a bowl, drizzle with soy sauce, and serve.

CAJUN-STYLE

Heat 2 tablespoons vegetable oil in a large skillet over high heat. Add 1 cup cooled cooked long-grain white rice, 2 ounces finely chopped cooked andouille sausage, ¼ cup minced white onion, ¼ cup minced green bell pepper, 1 minced garlic clove, and a pinch of cayenne and cook, stirring, until the rice is browned and crisp, about 5 minutes. Transfer to a bowl, top with sliced scallions and chopped fresh flat-leaf parsley, and serve.

SPANISH-STYLE

Heat 1 ounce finely chopped cured chorizo in a large skillet over high heat until its fat renders, 2 to 3 minutes. Add 1 cup cooled cooked short-grain white rice, ½ cup frozen peas, ¼ cup sliced jarred roasted red bell peppers, ½ teaspoon paprika, and 1 minced garlic clove and cook, stirring, until the rice is browned and crisp, about 5 minutes. Move the rice to one side of the skillet, add 5 coarsely chopped peeled and de-veined medium shrimp to the empty space, then cook until the shrimp are cooked through, 4 to 5 minutes, stirring just the shrimp once halfway through. Transfer the rice to a bowl, top with the shrimp, and serve.

MIDDLE EASTERN-STYLE

Heat 2 tablespoons vegetable oil in a large skillet over high heat. Add 1 thinly sliced shallot and a pinch of saffron (or ground turmeric) and cook, stirring, until golden brown, about 3 minutes. Stir in 1 cup cooled cooked white basmati rice, then lightly press the rice into a single layer in the skillet. Let cook, undisturbed, until the bottom of the rice is golden and crisp, 5 minutes. Break up the rice into bite-size chunks and cook, stirring, until all the rice is warmed through. Transfer to a bowl, top with chopped pistachios, pomegranate seeds, thinly sliced fresh mint leaves, and serve.

chinese-style

cajun-style

middle eastern-style

spanish-style

THAI QUINOA SALAD

SERVES 4

1 cup **vegetable stock**

1 cup **rainbow quinoa**, rinsed well

¼ cup **smooth peanut butter**

1 tablespoon low-sodium **soy sauce**

1 tablespoon grated **fresh ginger**

1 tablespoon **honey**

2 teaspoons **olive oil**

1 teaspoon **toasted sesame oil**

2 medium **carrots**, shredded

1 **red bell pepper**, finely chopped

1 **English cucumber**, quartered lengthwise, then thinly sliced crosswise

1 cup shredded **red cabbage**

½ cup cooked **edamame**

Thinly sliced **scallions** and finely chopped **roasted peanuts**, for garnish

4 **lime wedges**, for serving

If quinoa isn't already in your grain repertoire, prepare to become a convert. It's a high-protein, gluten-free grain with a delicate, nutty flavor, making it a perfect salad base. Cooking it in vegetable stock is a great way to infuse some extra flavor into it. This Thai-inspired peanut dressing is one of our favorites—and not just because it's easy to make with ingredients that might already be hanging out in your pantry. It's sweet, savory, and—thanks to the ginger—a little bit spicy. You might want to do yourself a favor and double the recipe.

1 Combine the stock and 1 cup water in a small saucepan and bring to a boil over high heat. Add the quinoa, cover, and reduce the heat to medium-low to maintain a simmer. Cook until the quinoa is tender, 15 to 20 minutes. Remove the pan from the heat and uncover; fluff the quinoa with a fork and let cool while you make the rest of the salad.

2 Whisk together the peanut butter, soy sauce, ginger, honey, olive oil, sesame oil, and ½ cup water in a small bowl until smooth. Set the dressing aside.

3 Divide the quinoa among four bowls. Working clockwise, arrange one-quarter each of the carrots, bell pepper, cucumber, cabbage, and edamame in separate piles around the edge of each bowl. Drizzle the dressing over each salad and top with scallions and peanuts. Serve each bowl with a lime wedge.

TEMPEH TACO SALAD

SALAD

2 tablespoons **olive oil**, plus more
as needed

1 (8-ounce) package **tempeh**, cut into
½-inch pieces

3 tablespoons low-sodium **soy sauce**

2 teaspoons **garlic powder**

2 teaspoons **chili powder**

1 teaspoon **ground cumin**

4 cups coarsely chopped **green-leaf
lettuce**

1 cup **cherry tomatoes**, halved

¾ cup canned **black beans**, drained and
rinsed

½ cup **corn kernels** (canned or fresh)

⅓ cup finely chopped **fresh cilantro**

⅓ cup finely chopped **red onion**

AVOCADO DRESSING

¼ cup **olive oil**

2 tablespoons fresh **lime juice**

1 ripe **avocado**

Kosher salt and **freshly ground black
pepper**

Tempeh might not have achieved the ubiquity of tofu, its
fellow soy protein, but we think it's time to give tempeh its
due. Firmer and chewier than tofu, tempeh adds a meatier
texture to foods and contains more protein and fiber—take
that, tofu! (Just kidding, we have enough soy-based love
to go around.) And no taco experience would be complete
without guac—or, in this case, a delicious avocado dressing
that brings all the flavors of guac to every nook and cranny
of your salad.

1. Make the salad: Heat the olive oil in a large saucepan over
medium heat. Once the oil begins to shimmer, add the
tempeh and cook, stirring and adding more oil as needed if
the pan gets dry, until golden brown, 6 to 8 minutes.

2. Reduce the heat to medium-low and stir in the soy sauce,
garlic powder, chili powder, and cumin. Cook, stirring
occasionally, until all the seasonings are well distributed and
the tempeh is well browned, about 5 minutes. Remove the
pan from the heat.

3. Divide the lettuce among four bowls. Working clockwise,
arrange one-quarter each of the tomatoes, black beans, corn,
cilantro, onion, and tempeh in separate piles around the edge
of each bowl.

4. Make the avocado dressing: In a blender, combine the olive
oil, lime juice, avocado, and ¼ cup water, season with salt and
pepper, and blend until smooth.

5. Pour the dressing over each salad and serve.

MIDDLE EASTERN PITA SALAD

SERVES 4

2 small **pitas**

½ cup plus 2 tablespoons **olive oil**

Kosher salt

⅓ cup **fresh lemon juice**

1 tablespoon **white wine vinegar**

2 teaspoons **ground sumac** or **lemon zest**

¼ teaspoon **ground allspice**

2 **garlic cloves**, minced

Freshly ground black pepper

2 medium heads **romaine** or **green-leaf lettuce**, coarsely chopped

1 medium **English cucumber**, quartered lengthwise, then coarsely chopped crosswise

2 cups **cherry tomatoes**, halved

5 **scallions**, thinly sliced

½ cup thinly sliced **radishes**

1 **red bell pepper**, finely chopped

1 cup coarsely chopped **fresh flat-leaf parsley**

½ cup coarsely chopped **fresh mint** leaves

Fattoush—a Lebanese bread salad made with toasted pita, tomatoes, radishes, and cucumber—is one of our favorites. After all, what's not to love about a bread salad, especially one that's full of delicious veggies, fresh herbs, and, of course, sumac, a spice with a bright, sour taste that's used in a lot of Middle Eastern and Mediterranean cuisine, including the spice blend za'atar. You can find it in Middle Eastern grocery stores, but if your grocery store has a good spice section, you might be able to find it there. In a pinch, you can swap in lemon zest.

1. Preheat the oven to 350°F.

2. Split the pitas in half to make 4 thin rounds. Place the pitas on a baking sheet, brush them all over with 2 tablespoons of the olive oil, and season with salt. Bake until the pitas are golden brown and crispy, 5 to 7 minutes.

3. Whisk together the remaining ½ cup olive oil, the lemon juice, vinegar, sumac, allspice, and garlic in a liquid measuring cup or small bowl and season with salt and black pepper.

4. Divide the lettuce among four bowls. Working clockwise, arrange one-quarter each of the cucumber, tomatoes, scallions, radishes, bell pepper, parsley, and mint in separate piles around the edge of each bowl.

5. Break the crispy pitas into small pieces, sprinkle them over each salad, and serve with the dressing alongside.

MOROCCAN TAGINE BOWL

SERVES 4

1 head **cauliflower**, cored and broken into florets (5 cups)

¼ cup plus 3 tablespoons **olive oil**

Kosher salt and **freshly ground black pepper**

4 small boneless, skinless **chicken breasts** (4 to 6 ounces each)

1½ teaspoons **ground coriander**

1½ teaspoons **sweet paprika**

2 **garlic cloves**, thinly sliced

10 ounces **baby spinach**

3 cups cooked **couscous**

½ cup **dried apricots**, quartered

½ cup sliced **almonds**, toasted

A classic Moroccan tagine is a stew of chicken or lamb, vegetables, dried fruits, nuts, and plenty of spices cooked to perfection in a cone-shaped clay pot (also called a tagine). But there's no need to buy your own tagine to make this tagine (still with us?)—a skillet will do just fine. You'll still get the bold flavors of coriander and paprika and the delicious combination of sweet and savory—yeah, you're a lean, mean tagine machine.

1 Preheat the oven to 400°F. Line a baking sheet with foil.

2 In a large bowl, toss the cauliflower with ¼ cup of the olive oil and season with salt and pepper. Spread the cauliflower out on the prepared baking sheet and bake until tender and golden brown, 35 to 40 minutes. Set the pan on a wire rack and let cool.

3 Meanwhile, heat a large skillet over medium-high heat. Brush the chicken with 2 tablespoons of the olive oil, then sprinkle with the coriander and paprika and season with salt and pepper. Place the chicken in the skillet and cook until cooked through and golden brown, 10 to 12 minutes, flipping once halfway through. Transfer the chicken to a cutting board and let rest for 10 minutes, then cut each breast crosswise into ½-inch-thick slices.

4 Return the skillet to medium-high heat and add the remaining 1 tablespoon olive oil. Add the garlic and cook, stirring, for 20 seconds. Add the spinach, season with salt and pepper, and cook, stirring often, until wilted and tender, 2 to 3 minutes. Remove the skillet from the heat.

5 Bring 2¼ cups of water to a boil in a medium pot over high heat. Add the couscous, cover, and let sit for 5 to 10 minutes. Once the water has been fully absorbed, fluff the couscous with a fork. Stir in the apricots, cover, and let sit for 5 minutes more, until the dried fruit is warmed.

6 Divide the couscous among four bowls. Top with the chicken, cauliflower, and spinach, sprinkle with the almonds, and serve.

ITALIAN MEATBALL AND WHITE BEAN BOWL

1 pint **cherry tomatoes** or **grape tomatoes**, halved

¼ cup lightly packed **fresh flat-leaf parsley**, finely chopped, plus more for serving

3 tablespoons **red wine vinegar**

1 tablespoon **honey**

1 small **shallot**, minced

Kosher salt and **freshly ground black pepper**

12 ounces **ground pork**

⅓ cup **Italian herb bread crumbs**

¼ cup shredded **low-moisture mozzarella cheese**

3 tablespoons **whole-milk ricotta cheese**

¼ cup grated **Parmesan cheese**, plus more for serving

1 large **egg**, lightly beaten

1 **garlic clove**, minced

4 tablespoons **olive oil**

2 cups **broccoli florets**

2 (15-ounce) cans **cannellini beans**, drained and rinsed

Sure, you've heard of spaghetti and meatballs, but there's a new iconic duo in town. Cannellini beans are a staple of Italian cuisine, so it seemed only natural to pair them with Italian meatballs. Instead of marinara, you'll make a no-cook tomato relish to tie it all together. Spaghetti and meatballs have nothing on this bowl—unless, of course, you're trying to re-create that scene from *L and the Tramp*. Even we have to admit that cannellini beans aren't so great for that.

1 Combine the tomatoes, parsley, vinegar, honey, and shallot in a medium bowl. Season with salt and pepper and stir to combine. Let the tomato relish stand at room temperature for at least 10 minutes or while you finish cooking.

2 Combine the pork, bread crumbs, mozzarella, ricotta, Parmesan, egg, and garlic in a large bowl. Season with salt and pepper and mix until evenly combined. Using your hands, pinch off golf ball–size pieces of the meat mixture and roll them into balls A . (You should have about 16 meatballs.)

3 Heat 2 tablespoons of the olive oil in a large skillet over medium-high heat. Add the meatballs in a single layer and cook, turning as needed, until golden brown on the outside and cooked through inside, 10 to 12 minutes B . Transfer the meatballs to a plate.

4 Return the skillet to medium heat and heat the remaining 2 tablespoons olive oil. Add the broccoli, season with salt and pepper, and toss to coat with the oil. Cook, undisturbed, until the bottom of the broccoli begins to char lightly, 3 to 4 minutes, then stir C . Cook the broccoli until just tender, 3 to 4 minutes more. Transfer the broccoli to a bowl and keep warm.

5 Return the skillet to medium heat and add the beans and
¼ cup water D . Bring to a simmer and cook, stirring,
until the beans are warmed through, about 2 minutes.
Remove the skillet from the heat and season the beans
with salt and pepper.

6 Divide the beans among four bowls and top with the
meatballs, tomato relish, and broccoli. Sprinkle with more
Parmesan and parsley and serve.

BEEF KEBAB BOWL
WITH CARROTS, ZUCCHINI, AND HERBED YOGURT

SERVES 4

1½ pounds boneless **beef sirloin**, cut into 1-inch chunks

½ cup finely chopped **fresh flat-leaf parsley**, plus more for serving

1 tablespoon **sweet paprika**

1 teaspoon **dried mint**

½ teaspoon **ground cumin**

½ teaspoon **ground coriander**

¼ teaspoon **ground allspice**

¼ teaspoon **ground cinnamon**

Kosher salt and **freshly ground black pepper**

1 cup **plain Greek yogurt**

2 tablespoons **fresh lemon juice**

3 tablespoons finely chopped **fresh mint** leaves

2 medium **carrots**, quartered lengthwise

1 medium **zucchini**, quartered lengthwise

3 tablespoons **olive oil**

3 cups cooked **farro**

We love to grill, whether the weather outside is amenable or not. These beef kebab bowls would be great as an unexpected main course at a summer barbecue (bratwurst who?), but you can also make them right on your stovetop in a grill pan. Food on a stick, meet food in a bowl: we have a feeling you two are going to get along.

1. Line a baking sheet with foil. Combine the beef, ¼ cup of the parsley, the paprika, mint, cumin, coriander, allspice, and cinnamon in a large bowl and season with 1 teaspoon each of salt and pepper. Mix until evenly combined. Skewer 3 or 4 pieces of beef onto each of 8 wooden or metal skewers and set them on the prepared baking sheet. Refrigerate the kebabs for at least 20 minutes.

2. Meanwhile, stir together the remaining ¼ cup parsley, the yogurt, lemon juice, and mint in a small bowl. Season the yogurt sauce with salt and pepper.

3. Heat a grill pan over high heat. Brush the carrots and zucchini with 1 tablespoon of the olive oil, season with salt and pepper, then place them on the hot pan and cook, flipping once halfway through, until the vegetables are golden brown and tender, 8 to 10 minutes. Transfer the vegetables to a cutting board and coarsely chop them.

4. Return the grill pan to medium-high heat. Brush the kebabs with the remaining 2 tablespoons olive oil and grill, turning as needed, until lightly charred and cooked through, 8 to 10 minutes. Remove the skewers from the grill pan.

5. Divide the farro among four bowls and top with the warm carrots and zucchini. Lay 2 kebabs in each bowl and top with the yogurt sauce. Sprinkle with more parsley and serve.

HEARTY FALL
HARVEST BOWL

4 bone-in, skin-on **chicken thighs**

Kosher salt and **freshly ground black pepper**

1 large **tart apple**, cored and cut into 12 wedges

1 pound **Brussels sprouts**, trimmed and halved

2 tablespoons **olive oil**

1 cup whole **pecans**

2 tablespoons **maple syrup**

⅛ teaspoon **cayenne**

3 cups cooked **brown rice**

2 ounces **goat cheese** or **blue cheese**, crumbled

Nothing says "fall" like a perfectly caramelized apple. Warm apples and Brussels sprouts, crispy chicken thighs, hearty brown rice, and candied pecans (tossed in the cleverly reserved chicken fat, naturally) combine to make this meal feel like a warm hug in bowl form. If only every hug were sprinkled with cheese!

1 Preheat the oven to 400°F. Line a baking sheet with parchment paper or foil.

2 Season the chicken thighs all over with salt and pepper, then place them in a cold large skillet, skin-side down. Place the skillet over medium heat and cook the chicken thighs, undisturbed, until the skin is deep golden brown and crisp, about 10 minutes. Using tongs, transfer the thighs to one side of the prepared baking sheet, skin-side up. Remove the skillet from the heat, reserving the rendered fat in the skillet.

3 Place the apple wedges and Brussels sprouts in a medium bowl, drizzle with the olive oil, and toss to coat. Season with salt and pepper, then spread them out on the opposite side of the baking sheet from the chicken. Bake until the apples and Brussels sprouts are caramelized and tender and the chicken is cooked through, about 20 minutes.

4 Meanwhile, heat the reserved fat in the skillet over medium-high heat. Add the pecans, season with salt and pepper, and cook, tossing, until toasted, 2 to 3 minutes. Remove the pan from the heat and stir in the maple syrup and cayenne, continuing to stir until the nuts are coated, about 1 minute. Transfer the nuts to a plate and let cool.

5 Remove the baking sheet from the oven and let the chicken rest for 10 minutes before serving.

6 Divide the rice among four bowls and top with the apples and sprouts. Remove the bone from each thigh, then slice the meat and the skin. Place a sliced thigh in each bowl, top with the pecans and goat cheese, and serve.

BLACK PEPPERED TOFU
RICE BOWL

1 (14-ounce) package **extra-firm tofu**, drained and cut into 1-inch cubes

1 tablespoon **kosher salt**, plus more as needed

3 tablespoons **vegetable oil**

12 ounces **green beans**, trimmed and halved

1 tablespoon **freshly ground black pepper**, plus more as needed

1 teaspoon **sugar**

3 **garlic cloves**, minced

2 large **scallions**, cut into ½-inch pieces

1 **serrano chile**, seeded (if desired) and thinly sliced

3 cups **cooked white rice**

8 **cremini mushrooms**, cleaned and very thinly shaved

Fresh cilantro leaves, for garnish

Tofu is like a flavor sponge: not much to taste on its own, but add some seasoning and aromatics, and oh, baby! Those porous little cubes will soak up all that deliciousness. This recipe uses more black pepper than you might be used to, transforming it from a background note to a front-and-center flavor. If you're a spice fan, leave the seeds in your serrano chile for some extra fire; if you like things a little milder, scrape them out.

1   Place the tofu in a large bowl and sprinkle evenly with the salt. Add boiling water to cover the tofu A , then stir gently until the salt has dissolved. Let the tofu soak for 15 minutes B . Drain the tofu and press it between layers of paper towels until there's no excess moisture C .

2   While the tofu soaks, heat the vegetable oil in a wok or large skillet over medium-high heat. Add the green beans, season with salt, and toss to coat with the oil. Cook, undisturbed, until the beans are lightly charred on the bottom, about 2 minutes, then stir D . Cook until the beans are just tender, about 2 minutes more. Using tongs, transfer the beans to paper towels to drain.

3   Return the wok to high heat. Add the tofu to the oil left in the wok and cook, tossing occasionally, until light golden brown, about 5 minutes. Reduce the heat to medium-high, add the pepper, sugar, garlic, scallions, and chile E , and cook, tossing often, until the spices are fragrant and the tofu is golden brown and crisp, 2 to 3 minutes more F .

4   Divide the rice among four plates and top with the hot tofu. Place the green beans and shaved mushrooms next to the tofu, sprinkle with cilantro, and serve.

A

B

C

D

E

F

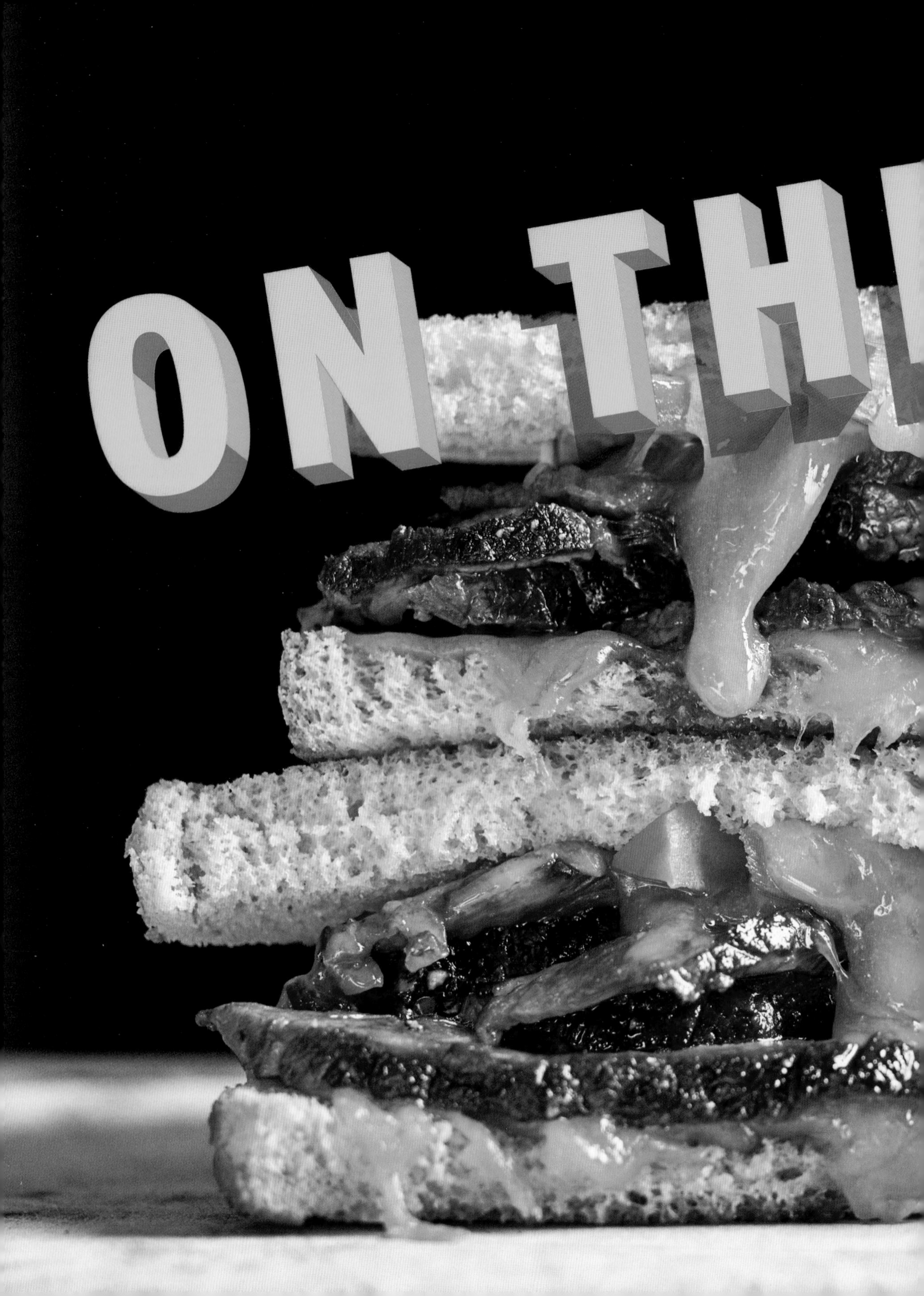
ON TH

FRITTATA SANDWICHES

These frittata sandwiches might remind you of a certain fast food breakfast favorite, but since we're culinary rebels, we think they also make for a pretty tasty lunch, dinner, or snack. What can we say? We strive for egg-cellence at each meal! Whip up a batch and freeze them individually, then reheat in the microwave or oven. Frittasty!

SERVES 4

‹• • • • • • • • • • • • • •›

1 tablespoon **olive oil**

8 large **eggs**

¼ cup **whole milk**

2 tablespoons finely chopped **fresh chives**

Kosher salt and **freshly ground black pepper**

4 **English muffins**, split

4 slices **Cheddar cheese**

½ cup jarred roasted **red bell pepper** strips

1 cup lightly packed **arugula leaves**

¼ cup whole-grain **Dijon mustard**

1 Preheat the oven to 350°F. Brush an 8-inch square baking dish with the olive oil.

2 In a medium bowl, whisk together the eggs, milk, and chives. Season with salt and pepper. Pour the eggs into the prepared baking dish and bake until puffed and just set in the middle, about 30 minutes. Set the dish on a wire rack and cut the frittata into 4 squares in the pan.

3 Toast the English muffin halves, then place a frittata square on the bottom half of each muffin. Top each with a slice of Cheddar and divide the red pepper strips and arugula evenly among them. Spread 1 tablespoon of the mustard evenly inside each muffin top. Close the sandwiches, wrap in foil, and serve.

EAT IT FOUR DIFFERENT WAYS

MAKE IT

MEAL PREP

day ①

Serve with half an avocado drizzled
with olive oil, seasoned with lime
juice, sea salt, and black pepper.

day ②

Add veggie sausage patties to each
sandwich for extra protein.

Serve with a peeled orange or a cup
of fruit salad.

Pair the sandwich with a green juice
or a smoothie.

day ④

day ③

CHICKEN SALAD PITAS

SERVES 4

3 cups shredded **rotisserie chicken**

⅔ cup **low-fat plain Greek yogurt**

½ cup finely chopped **celery**

1½ tablespoons **sweet or dill pickle relish**

1 tablespoon **Dijon mustard**

1 teaspoon **garlic powder**

½ teaspoon **sweet paprika**

1 **scallion**, thinly sliced

Kosher salt and **freshly ground black pepper**

4 leaves **romaine or green-leaf lettuce**

4 **pitas**, toasted

12 **cherry tomatoes** or **grape tomatoes**, halved

We love mayo, but sometimes we want to lighten up. Enter: Greek yogurt. It has a similar tang and texture to mayo, but with less fat and sodium, fewer calories, and more protein. This healthier version of a classic chicken salad will keep you full without weighing you down.

1 Combine the chicken, yogurt, celery, relish, mustard, garlic powder, paprika, and scallion in a large bowl. Season with salt and pepper and mix until well combined.

2 Divide the lettuce among the pitas, then fill each with one-quarter of the chicken salad. Divide the tomatoes among the pitas, then wrap them up in foil and serve.

LEFTOVER TURKEY— SALAD SANDWICHES

⅓ cup **olive oil**

2 tablespoons **white wine vinegar**

2 tablespoons **fresh lemon juice**

1 tablespoon finely chopped **fresh dill**

2 teaspoons **Dijon mustard**, plus more for serving

1 pound leftover cooked **turkey**, chopped into ½-inch pieces

¼ cup **sour cream**

½ large **white onion**, finely chopped

Kosher salt and **freshly ground black pepper**

1 small head **Little Gem lettuce**, leaves separated, cleaned, and dried

8 slices **white or whole-wheat sandwich bread**

8 slices **Swiss cheese**

It's well-established that the best part of Thanksgiving is the leftovers. These sandwiches take that leftover turkey to the next level with tangy vinaigrette, sour cream, and perfectly dressed lettuce. No matter what season it is, we'll always give thanks for a tasty sandwich.

1 Whisk together the olive oil, vinegar, lemon juice, dill, and mustard in a medium bowl until smooth. Transfer 3 tablespoons of the vinaigrette to a small bowl and set aside. Add the turkey, sour cream, and onion to the vinaigrette in the medium bowl and stir until evenly combined. Season with salt and pepper.

2 Add the lettuce leaves to the small bowl of vinaigrette, season with salt and pepper, and gently toss the lettuce leaves until evenly coated with the vinaigrette.

3 Spread mustard to your liking over 4 slices of the bread. Divide the turkey salad among the slices and top each with 2 slices of the cheese and some of the dressed lettuce leaves. Top with the remaining bread slices, wrap the sandwiches in foil, and serve.

CHICKEN, BROCCOLI, AND CHEDDAR POCKETS

2 sheets store-bought **puff pastry** (from one 17.3-ounce box), thawed overnight in the fridge

½ cup store-bought **Alfredo sauce**, plus more for serving

1 cup frozen chopped **broccoli**, steamed and cooled

¾ cup shredded **rotisserie chicken**

¾ cup shredded **Cheddar cheese**

1 large **egg**, beaten with 1 tablespoon water, for egg wash

It's a fact of life: not all meals can take place at a nicely set table with no phones, no distractions, and no time constraints. In fact, sometimes meals must be eaten in the passenger seat of a car, or sitting at a desk, or even walking down the street. It happens! And when it does, you're going to want these chicken-broccoli-cheddar pockets in your corner. Eating a well-balanced meal? You can do that one-handed!

1. Preheat the oven to 400°F. Line a baking sheet with parchment paper or foil.

2. On a cutting board, cut each puff pastry sheet into 6 rectangles A . Place 6 of the rectangles on the prepared baking sheet.

3. Spread 1 heaping tablespoon of the Alfredo sauce on each rectangle on the baking sheet, leaving a ½-inch border B . Top the sauce with the broccoli, chicken, and Cheddar C , dividing them evenly among the pastry rectangles D .

4. Place a second rectangle of pastry on top of each filled rectangle on the baking sheet, covering the filling E . Press the edges to seal and crimp with a fork. Brush the pastry with the egg wash F .

5. Bake until the pastry pockets are flaky and golden brown, 20 to 25 minutes. Remove the baking sheet from the oven and let the pockets cool for 10 minutes before serving.

6. Wrap each pocket in foil and serve with a small cup of extra Alfredo sauce for dipping.

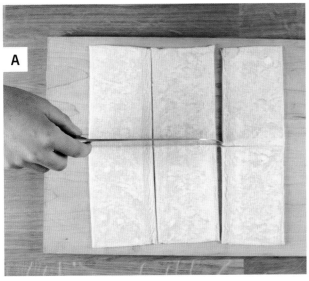

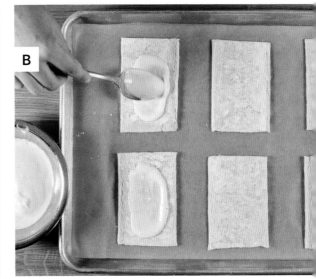

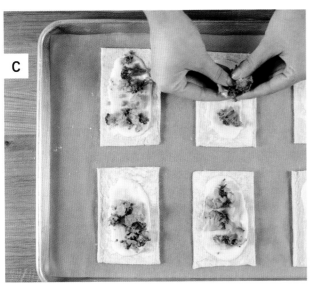

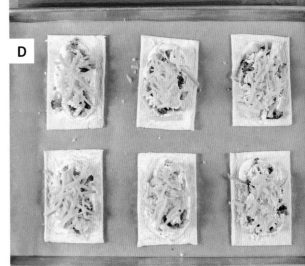

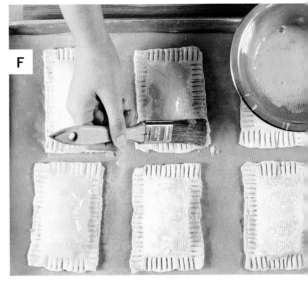

BUFFALO CHICKPEA WRAPS

2 tablespoons **olive oil**

2 (15-ounce) cans **chickpeas**, drained, rinsed, and dried thoroughly

½ cup **mild hot sauce**, such as Frank's RedHot

1 teaspoon **garlic powder**

Kosher salt and **freshly ground black pepper**

⅔ cup **hummus**

2 tablespoons **fresh lemon juice**

4 leaves **romaine or green-leaf lettuce**

4 burrito-size **flour tortillas**

4 thick slices vine-ripe or heirloom **tomato**

¼ cup thinly sliced **red onion**

Buffalo wings are a classic game-day snack, so when we were challenged to create a vegan dish that preserves their flavors while elevating them to full-on meal status, we thought, *Game on*. Browning the chickpeas lends them a delicious crunch, and a hummus-based sauce is the perfect vegan, protein-rich alternative to ranch or blue cheese dressing. Score!

1 Heat the olive oil in a large saucepan over medium heat. Once the oil begins to shimmer, add the chickpeas and cook, stirring, until lightly browned, 4 to 5 minutes. Add the hot sauce and garlic powder, season with salt and pepper. Cook, stirring, until the sauce thickens and the chickpeas are well browned, about 5 minutes. Remove the pan from the heat.

2 Whisk together the hummus, lemon juice, and 1 tablespoon water in a small bowl or liquid measuring cup until smooth.

3 Place a lettuce leaf in the center of each tortilla. Top the lettuce with one-quarter of the chickpeas, 1 tomato slice, and one-quarter of the onion. Pour one-quarter of the dressing over each.

4 Fold in the sides of each tortilla and roll it up around the filling like a burrito. Cut the roll in half crosswise, then wrap each whole wrap in foil and serve.

STEAK AND CHEDDAR GRILLED CHEESE SANDWICHES

WITH QUICK-PICKLED CARROTS

1 cup **white wine vinegar**

1 tablespoon **kosher salt**

1 tablespoon **whole black peppercorns**

2 teaspoons **crushed red pepper flakes**

4 medium **carrots**, cut into ½-inch-wide sticks

2 **garlic cloves**, peeled and smashed

1 large **shallot**, thinly sliced

1 tablespoon **vegetable oil**

8 ounces **flank steak**

Kosher salt and **freshly ground black pepper**

2 tablespoons **unsalted butter**

4 slices **sourdough bread**

2 cups shredded **sharp Cheddar cheese** (8 ounces)

We're so sure you'll love this grilled cheese, we'd "steak" our reputation on it. How come? Three words: quick-pickled carrots, which are absolutely delicious on everything from burgers to salads to tacos. Their sour tang works particularly well here by cutting the richness of the steak and cheese. A surefire sandwich enhancer with the word *quick* right there in the name? Doesn't get any better than that.

1 Combine the vinegar, salt, peppercorns, red pepper flakes, carrots, garlic, shallot, and 1¼ cups water in a medium saucepan A . Bring to a boil over high heat and cook, stirring, for 1 minute. Remove from the heat and let the carrots cool to room temperature, about 20 minutes, before using. (If not using immediately, transfer the carrots and their brine to an airtight container and refrigerate. They will keep for up to 2 weeks.)

2 Meanwhile, heat the vegetable oil in a large cast-iron skillet over high heat. Season the steak with salt and pepper, add it to the skillet, and cook until golden brown on the outside and medium-rare inside, 6 to 8 minutes B , flipping once halfway through. Transfer to a cutting board and let rest for 10 minutes.

3 Return the skillet to medium heat and add the butter. Once the butter has melted, add 2 slices of the bread, top each with ½ cup of the Cheddar, and cook, undisturbed, until the bread is golden brown and toasted on the bottom, about 3 minutes.

4 Thinly slice the steak across the grain. Top each bread slice in the skillet with half the sliced steak C , then top each with ½ cup of the remaining cheese D and a slice of bread. Flip the sandwiches E , cover with the lid, and cook until the cheese has fully melted in the sandwiches and the other side of the bread is golden brown and toasted, 2 to 3 minutes more.

5 Transfer the sandwiches to a cutting board and wrap each in foil. Serve the sandwiches with the carrots on the side.

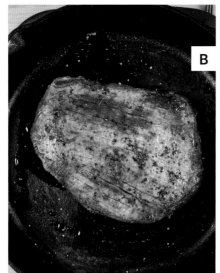

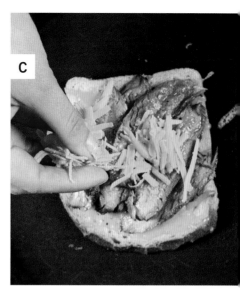

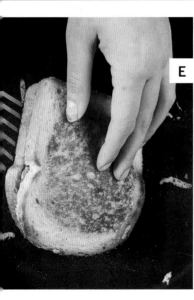

MOROCCAN-STYLE TUNA BAGUETTE SANDWICHES

SERVES 4 TO 6

WITH OLIVES AND PEPPERS

3 tablespoons **olive oil**

1 small **yellow onion**, finely chopped

1 small **red bell pepper**, finely chopped

¼ cup **harissa paste**

2 **garlic cloves**, minced

1 (15-ounce) can whole peeled **tomatoes**, crushed by hand in their juices

Kosher salt and **freshly ground black pepper**

2 **French baguettes** (each about 2 feet long)

1½ cups drained **olive oil–packed tuna** (from two 5-ounce cans)

½ cup pitted **kalamata olives**

¼ cup **capers**, drained and rinsed

4 **pepperoncini peppers**, drained, stemmed, and thinly sliced

½ small **English cucumber**, thinly sliced

You've caught us red-handed in our efforts to make everyone a harissa convert. Harissa paste is a bright red North African spice paste made with roasted red peppers, chiles, garlic, and spices. It's widely used in traditional Tunisian and Moroccan dishes, but it's also a perfect way to add a spicy-smoky flavor to roasted veggies (as you'll do here), salad dressings, and even eggs. Try this sandwich, and you'll see why we think you're better off red.

1 Preheat the oven to 375°F.

2 Heat the olive oil in a large skillet over medium-high heat. Add the onion and bell pepper and cook, stirring occasionally, until tender, 6 to 8 minutes. Add the harissa and garlic and cook, stirring occasionally, until fragrant, about 2 minutes. Pour in the tomatoes and their juices and cook, stirring often, until the mixture comes to a simmer. Reduce the heat to medium-low to maintain a simmer and cook, stirring, until the liquid reduces to the consistency of a thick sauce, about 8 minutes. Remove the skillet from the heat and season the sauce with salt and black pepper.

3 Split each baguette lengthwise from end to end, leaving one long side attached. Place the baguettes on a baking sheet and bake until toasted and crispy at the edges, about 5 minutes. Remove the baguettes from the oven.

4 Divide the tomato sauce between the baguettes and spread it all over the insides. Break up the tuna into bite-size chunks and divide it between the baguettes. Top each with olives, capers, and pepperoncini slices, then layer on the cucumber. Close the baguettes and cut each in half or into thirds. Wrap the sandwiches in foil and serve.

EGGPLANT "BACON," LETTUCE, AND TOMATO

¼ cup **olive oil**

3 tablespoons **tamari** or **coconut aminos** (or **soy sauce**, if you're not vegan)

2 tablespoons **vegan Worcestershire sauce** (or regular, if you're not vegan)

2 tablespoons **maple syrup**

1 tablespoon **smoked paprika**

1 teaspoon **freshly ground black pepper**

½ teaspoon **garlic powder**

1 medium **eggplant**, ends trimmed, quartered lengthwise

Flaky sea salt

8 slices **sandwich bread**

Vegan mayonnaise

8 slices vine-ripe **tomato**

4 leaves **iceberg or green-leaf lettuce**

One of the things that makes bacon so delicious is its distinctive smokiness, so when devising a vegan version of the classic BLT sandwich, we decided to substitute eggplant, a vegetable that shares that smoky quality, especially when you add a little paprika to the mix. Slicing it thinly with a mandoline will ensure it crisps up perfectly, and tamari, Worcestershire, and maple syrup will help give your eggplant bacon (or "fake-on," if you will) the ideal savory sweetness.

1 Preheat the oven to 350°F. Line two rimmed baking sheets with parchment paper.

2 Whisk together the olive oil, tamari, Worcestershire, maple syrup, paprika, pepper, and garlic powder in a medium bowl.

3 Using a mandoline or very sharp knife, thinly slice the eggplant lengthwise, about $\frac{1}{16}$ inch thick so it resembles bacon. Add the eggplant to the bowl with the sauce and toss to coat completely. Arrange the eggplant slices on the prepared baking sheets, dividing them evenly.

4 Bake until the slices are golden brown and crisp, about 30 minutes. Set the baking sheets on wire racks, sprinkle the eggplant with flaky sea salt, and let cool for 5 minutes.

5 Toast the sandwich bread, if you like, and spread one side of each with as much mayonnaise as you like. Place 2 tomato slices and 1 lettuce leaf on each of 4 slices of the bread. Top each with one-quarter of the eggplant bacon and another slice of bread, mayonnaise-side down. Wrap the sandwiches in foil and serve.

QUICK-AND-EASY

FRUIT SALADS

In a chapter devoted to snacks and noshes, we couldn't neglect possibly the greatest snack of all: fresh fruit. These easy-breezy salads represent some of our favorite fruits, and as you'll see, we pretty much let them shine on their own. A touch of sugar, a pinch of salt (seriously, it's delish), a bit of honey—it doesn't take much to turn a fruit into a vibrant, enticing presentation for any occasion. Let's get a round of apple-ause for fruit!

EAT IT FOUR DIFFERENT WAYS

RED BERRY

In a serving bowl, mix together 4 sliced hulled strawberries, 8 raspberries, 8 halved red grapes, and 8 halved pitted cherries. Toss with 1 teaspoon sugar and a pinch of kosher salt, if you like. Serve cold.

MELON AND MINT

In a serving bowl, mix together ½ cup chopped (1-inch pieces) ripe honeydew melon, ½ cup chopped (1-inch pieces) ripe cantaloupe, and ½ cup chopped (1-inch pieces) peeled cucumber. Sprinkle with 2 tablespoons thinly sliced fresh mint leaves, 1 teaspoon sugar, and a pinch of kosher salt, and toss to combine before serving.

TROPICAL

In a serving bowl, mix together ½ cup chopped (1-inch pieces) pineapple, 1 small orange (peeled and cut into segments), and ½ cup chopped (1-inch-pieces) mango. Drizzle with honey and sprinkle with toasted coconut flakes, if you like.

AUTUMN SPICE

In a serving bowl, mix together ½ tart apple (cored and cut into ½-inch pieces), ½ ripe pear (cored and cut into ½-inch pieces), 1 tablespoon maple syrup, 1 teaspoon fresh lemon juice, and a pinch each of ground cinnamon and kosher salt. Serve with a dollop of plain yogurt on top, if you like.

red berry

tropical

melon and mint

autumn spice

COCONUT CHIA PUDDING

WITH ORANGES, PINEAPPLE, AND DRIED CHERRIES

1½ cups **sweetened vanilla-flavored almond milk**

½ cup **chia seeds**

½ cup **dried cherries**

2 tablespoons **maple syrup**

½ teaspoon **kosher salt**

1 **orange**, peeled and segmented

¼ **pineapple**, cored and finely chopped

Toasted coconut flakes, for garnish (optional)

If you had told us ten years ago that chia seed pudding would become one of our favorite breakfasts, we probably would have been … confused, honestly! Chia? Like the pets? So if you haven't RSVP'd to the chia party yet, we understand. Luckily, this pudding is the perfect place to start. Thick, creamy, and—thanks to the fresh orange and pineapple—oh, so refreshing, this vegan treat will make you a convert to the charms of chia.

1 Stir together the almond milk, chia seeds, cherries, maple syrup, and salt in a large bowl. Cover the bowl with plastic wrap and refrigerate for at least 6 hours or up to overnight.

2 Stir the chia pudding well, then divide it among four serving cups. Divide the orange segments and chopped pineapple evenly among the cups. Serve immediately, sprinkled with toasted coconut, if desired, or cover with plastic wrap and store refrigerated for up to 5 days (wait until just before serving to sprinkle with coconut).

MAPLE-CINNAMON TRAIL MIX

MAKES 4

1 cup **raw hulled pumpkin seeds** (5 ounces)

1 cup **raw walnuts**, chopped (3½ ounces)

1 cup **raw unsalted whole almonds** (5 ounces)

3 tablespoons **maple syrup**

1½ teaspoons **kosher salt**

1 teaspoon **ground cinnamon**

1 cup **dried unsweetened cranberries**

Whether you're on a mountain trail or on the figurative trail of life, this snack will provide the fuel you need to keep on moving. A little maple syrup and some dried cranberries add just the right amount of sweetness, while kosher salt and cinnamon balance out the flavors. This munchable mix is perfect as a solo artist, eaten with your hands, or as a duet with unsweetened Greek yogurt.

1 Preheat the oven to 350°F. Line a rimmed baking sheet with parchment paper or foil.

2 Combine the pumpkin seeds, walnuts, almonds, maple syrup, salt, and cinnamon in a large bowl and toss to combine. Spread the mixture over the prepared baking sheet in an even layer (set the bowl aside—no need to clean it). Bake, stirring every 5 minutes, until the nuts are toasted and the mixture is mostly dry, about 20 minutes.

3 Transfer the mixture back to the bowl and let cool completely, tossing every few minutes, for about 10 minutes. Stir in the cranberries.

4 Store the trail mix in an airtight container at room temperature for up to 1 week.

PEANUT BUTTER BLUEBERRY
FROZEN YOGURT CUPS

1 cup **nonfat plain Greek yogurt**

1 tablespoon **honey**

¼ cup plus 2 tablespoons **smooth peanut butter**

½ cup **fresh or frozen blueberries**

A delicious frozen treat with no added sugar and plenty of protein? *Fro* yeah! These frozen yogurt bites will satisfy your ice cream craving, and they're so full of good-for-you ingredients (oh, hey there, antioxidants!) that you don't have to save them till after your meal. Because as a very wise saying goes, "Life is uncertain; eat dessert first."

1 Line 6 wells of a muffin tin with paper liners. Stir together the yogurt and honey in a small bowl. Spoon 3 tablespoons of the mixture into the prepared wells of the muffin tin.

2 Place the peanut butter in a microwave-safe bowl and microwave on high until slightly softened, about 15 seconds. Spoon 1 tablespoon of the softened peanut butter into each yogurt cup. Divide the blueberries among the yogurt cups.

3 Freeze the yogurt cups until solid, about 2 hours, before serving. The cups will keep in the freezer in an airtight container for up to a month.

VEGAN BANANA
ICE CREAM SANDWICHES

3 **very ripe bananas**, peeled

¼ cup **non-dairy milk**

1 teaspoon **vanilla extract**

¼ teaspoon **kosher salt**

16 thin **chocolate cookies** at least 2 inches in diameter, such as Nabisco Famous Chocolate Wafers

Bananas are nature's ice cream, so we've honored them in the best way we know how: blending them up and putting them between cookies. (There's no greater honor than being cookie sandwiched, honestly.) These cookie bites are as simple as they are delicious—and they're a great way to use up any brown bananas you've got lying around.

1. Line a baking sheet with parchment paper. Cut the bananas crosswise into coins and arrange them on the prepared baking sheet A . Freeze until the banana slices are frozen solid, at least 2 hours or up to overnight.

2. In a food processor or blender B , combine the frozen banana slices, milk, vanilla, and salt and process until smooth C . Scrape the "ice cream" into a small loaf pan and freeze until solid, at least 2 hours or up to overnight.

3. Arrange half the cookies on a baking sheet, bottom-sides up. Using a 1½-ounce ice cream scoop or a ¼-cup measuring cup (don't fill it quite to the top if using a measuring cup), scoop ice cream onto each cookie on the baking sheet D . Sandwich each with another cookie and store in the freezer in an airtight container until ready to serve, up to 3 days.

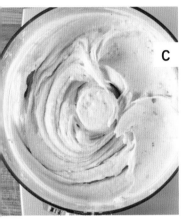

OATMEAL RAISIN
ENERGY BITES

MAKES
12 BITES

¼ cup **almond butter**

¼ cup **honey**

½ teaspoon **ground cinnamon**

½ teaspoon **vanilla extract**

Pinch of **kosher salt**

1 cup **old-fashioned rolled oats**

¼ cup **raisins**

¼ cup finely chopped **pecans**

Three-o'clock slump, prepare to be vanquished! One of these energy bites is enough to perk you up and see you through to quitting time (or, as we like to think of it, the start of your next adventure). They're a perfect alternative to energy bars, with no hidden ingredients—because, you know, you're the one making them—and they'll satisfy your sweet tooth without inducing a sugar coma.

1 Stir together the almond butter, honey, cinnamon, vanilla, and salt in a large bowl until smooth. Add the oats, raisins, and pecans and stir until evenly combined. Refrigerate the mixture until solidified, about 30 minutes.

2 Using a tablespoon, portion out heaping spoonfuls of the mixture and roll them into balls; you should have about 12 balls. Transfer the balls to a plate, cover, and refrigerate until ready to serve. The balls will keep in the fridge for up to a week.

BROWNIE BITES

2 cups **all-purpose flour**

1 teaspoon **baking powder**

½ cup **unsweetened Dutch-process cocoa powder**

2 cups lightly packed **fresh spinach** (2 ounces)

½ cup **honey**

½ cup **plain Greek yogurt**

1 tablespoon **vanilla extract**

2 large **eggs**

1 medium ripe **banana**, mashed

1 small ripe **avocado**, halved, pitted, peeled, and mashed

½ cup **semisweet chocolate chips**

These are the sneakiest brownies around—and that's a very good thing. Spinach and avocado don't sound like they belong in a dessert, but we like to think of these bites as stealthy-healthy: full of fruit and veggies, but with that perfect fudgy texture (thanks to the banana and avocado) and the chocolatey taste every good brownie needs. We're not saying it's magic, but let's just say we wouldn't be *too* surprised to find these served alongside the pumpkin juice at a certain wizarding school.

1 Preheat the oven to 350°F. Line a 12-cup muffin tin with paper liners.

2 Whisk together the flour, baking powder, and cocoa powder in a large bowl.

3 In a blender, combine the spinach, honey, yogurt, vanilla, eggs, banana, and avocado and puree until very smooth. Pour the wet ingredients into the dry ingredients and stir with a spatula until just combined. Stir in the chocolate chips.

4 Using a 2-ounce ice cream scoop or a ¼-cup measuring cup, fill the prepared muffin tin with heaping scoops of the batter. Bake until a toothpick inserted into the center of each brownie comes out clean (there may be some melted chocolate from the chips), 20 to 25 minutes.

5 Set the muffin tin on a wire rack and let the brownie bites cool completely in the tin before serving. The bites will keep, refrigerated in an airtight container, for up to 3 days.

CHOCOLATE-DIPPED RICE CAKE
"CANDY BAR" BITES

MAKES 32 PIECES

12 ounces **dark chocolate chips** (2 cups)

3 tablespoons **refined coconut oil**

1 cup finely chopped **honey-roasted peanuts**, **hazelnuts**, or **pistachios**, **freeze-dried strawberries or blueberries**, or **toasted coconut flakes** (or a mix of your favorites)

8 **rice cakes**

Flaky sea salt

If you've ever negotiated Halloween candy trades, you know that puffed rice and chocolate are a winning combination. The humble rice cake is a perfect shortcut to getting all-important crispiness. Adding coconut oil to your chocolate thins it, making it easier to use as a coating for your rice cakes. These bites are a perfect vehicle for our favorite thing: toppings! Try one of our suggestions, mix a few together, or go mad-candy-scientist and invent your own genius combinations!

1 Place the chocolate chips and coconut oil in a medium microwave-safe bowl. Microwave at 50 percent power for 5 minutes, stopping and stirring every 1 minute, until melted and the mixture is smooth. Transfer the chocolate to a 2-cup liquid measuring cup or tall glass for easy dipping.

2 Line a tray or baking sheet with foil. Spread your topping(s) of choice out on a plate. Break each rice cake into 4 pieces, then dip half of each piece in the chocolate, letting the excess drip off. While the chocolate is still warm, dip the pieces in the topping(s) to coat. Set the dipped pieces on the foil-lined tray or baking sheet and refrigerate until the chocolate sets, about 5 minutes, before serving.

ACKNOWLEDGMENTS

Contributing Producers

Tiffany Lo
Claire Nolan
Alix Traeger
Crystal Hatch
Rachel Gaewski
Katie Aubin
Chris Salicrup
Merle O'Neal
Jordan Kenna
Gwenaelle Le Cochennec
Alvin Zhou
Robin Broadfoot
Ellie Holland
Alexa D'Argenio
Marissa Buie
Julie Klink
Joey Firoben
Camille Bergerson
Kahnita Wilkerson
Emily DePaula
Ashley McCollum

Bloggers, chefs, and recipe developers who inspired some of the recipes in this book:

- Shrimp-and-Pork Egg Rolls — Souped Up Recipes
- Taco-Night Crunch Wrap— Twisted
- Watermelon Salad with Spinach and Mango—Healthy Women
- Middle Eastern Pita Salad— The Mediterranean Dish
- Buffalo Chickpea Wraps— Minimalist Baker

Styling and Photography

Lauren Volo
Monica Pierini
Maeve Sheridan
Leila Clifford
Andie McMahon
Christina Zhang
Erica Santiago
Veronica Spera

Everyone at Clarkson Potter

Amanda Englander
Gabrielle Van Tassel
Stephanie Huntwork
Sonia Persad
Jan Derevjanik
Mark McCauslin
Ivy McFadden
Derek Gullino
Neil Spitkovsky
Nick Patton
Merri Ann Morrell
Kate Tyler
Erica Gelbard
Windy Dorresteyn
Stephanie Davis
Aaron Wehner
Doris Cooper
Jill Flaxman

Original Recipe Developer

Ben Mims

Recipe Tester

Susan Phuong My Vu

INDEX